UNIVERSITY TREATISE SERIES

ASSIGNMENTS TO
BARKAN, BINTLIFF, AND WHISNER'S

Fundamentals of Legal Research

and

Legal Research Illustrated

TENTH EDITIONS

by

SUSAN T. PHILLIPS
Professor of Law
Director, Dee J. Kelly Law Library
Texas A&M University School of Law

WENDY N. LAW
Associate Professor of Law
Head of Collection Development
Dee J. Kelly Law Library
Texas A&M University School of Law

JOAN E. STRINGFELLOW
Instructional Associate Professor of Law
Head of Technical and Electronic Services
Dee J. Kelly Law Library
Texas A&M University School of Law

FOUNDATION
PRESS

© 2009 By THOMSON REUTERS/FOUNDATION PRESS
© 2015 LEG, Inc. d/b/a West Academic
    444 Cedar Street, Suite 700
    St. Paul, MN 55101
    1-877-888-1330

West, West Academic Publishing, and West Academic are trademarks of West Publishing Corporation, used under license.

Printed in the United States of America

ISBN: 978-1-60930-057-9

TABLE OF CONTENTS

STUDENT INTRODUCTION

All attorneys are charged with knowing the fundamentals of legal research. To reach this objective, you must learn what research tools are available, the content of each tool, and how to use each tool. *Fundamentals of Legal Research* (10th ed.) and *Legal Research Illustrated* (10th ed.) are the narrative resources for this information. However to master legal research skills, you must learn to use the tools. To learn, you must practice and then practice some more. The assignments in this book provide practice in using the tools with the goal that you will gain the required fundamentals needed for the profession.

The first fifteen assignments are organized to correspond to the chapters in *Fundamentals of Legal Research* (10th ed.) and *Legal Research Illustrated* (10th ed.) that cover legal research resources most law students learn about in their first year. Each assignment has six variations (A-F), allowing you to repeat the exercise until you have mastered the skill. If working in print, be cooperative with your classmates and share the books. In addition, we give you an example exercise complete with answers at the beginning of each assignment. We provide these examples for two reasons: First, the sample answers allow you to see what your answers should look like—eliminating anxiety as to how the answers should look. For most first year students, legal research is like a foreign language and knowing the format for your answers should help you focus on the substance. Second, the sample answers provide you an opportunity to walk through a problem with the answers given so you can duplicate the research. We want you to learn to conduct effective and efficient legal research with as few distractions as possible.

The questions in these assignments ask you to locate information. Sometimes we direct you to a specific source and other times we do not. When we do not, you typically have a number of sources from which to choose to use depending on your library's resources. Refer to the corresponding chapter in *Fundamentals of Legal Research* or *Legal Research Illustrated* for information on possible sources. In most exercises, we wrote the questions to be "media neutral," that is, they can be completed in either print resources or in electronic resources depending on the resources available at your library as well as the preference of your instructor. In a few instances, we direct you to an online resource.

The last assignment, Assignment Sixteen, contains six fact situations for you to research using the skills and resources you learned in the previous assignments. These problems are designed to be researched in your jurisdiction.

Read the special instructions at the beginning of each assignment. These instructions provide guidance for citation and to the resources that we used to write the questions as well as the possible resources that you can use to answer the questions. For citation, use *The Bluebook: A Uniform System of Citation* (Columbia Law Review Ass'n et al. eds., 20th ed. 2015).

Although we tried to eliminate mistakes, drafting errors do occur for which we apologize. In addition, it is a usual occurrence in legal publishing, both in print and online, for legal research resources to change with updates. All of our questions have been written to help you locate information. If you find you are spending an inordinate amount of time on a question, seek research help. The most important resources for completing these problems are your instructor, the *Fundamentals of Legal Research* or the *Legal Research Illustrated* book, and your librarian. If you do not understand a research tool or concept after reading the book, ask a librarian. We are here to help.

Susan T. Phillips
Professor of Law
Director of the Law Library
Dee J. Kelly Law Library
Texas A&M University School of Law

Wendy N. Law
Associate Professor of Law
Head of Collection Development
Dee J. Kelly Law Library
Texas A&M University School of Law

Joan E. Stringfellow
Instructional Associate Professor of Law
Head of Technical and Electronic Services
Dee J. Kelly Law Library
Texas A&M University School of Law

FUNDAMENTALS OF LEGAL RESEARCH CHAPTERS/ASSIGNMENTS
CORRELATION CHART

LEGAL RESEARCH ILLUSTRATED CHAPTERS/ASSIGNMENTS
CORRELATION CHART

Chapter	Assignments
1: An Introduction to Legal Research	None
2: The Legal Research Process	None
3: Communicating Research Results through Writing	None
4: Court Reports and the National Reporter System	One
5: Federal Court Reports	Two
6: State Court Reports	Three
7: Digests for Court Reports	Four
8: Constitutional Law and the Supreme Court of the United States	Five
9: Federal Legislation	Six
10: Federal Legislative Histories and Legislative Materials	Seven
11: State and Municipal Legislation	Eight
12: Court Rules and Procedures	Nine
13: Administrative Law	Ten
14: Topical Services	None
15: Citators	Eleven
16: Legal Encyclopedias	Twelve
17: American Law Reports (A.L.R.)	Thirteen
18: Legal Periodicals and Indexes	Fourteen
19: Treatises, Restatements, Uniform Laws, and Model Acts	Fifteen
20: Practice Materials and Other Resources	None
21: Public International Law	None
22: Electronic Legal Research	None
23: Legal Citation Form	None

UNIVERSITY TREATISE SERIES

ASSIGNMENTS TO
BARKAN, BINTLIFF, AND WHISNER'S

Fundamentals of Legal Research

and

Legal Research Illustrated

TENTH EDITIONS

Assignment One
Chapter 4
JUDICIAL OPINIONS AND THEIR SEGMENTS

GOALS:
• Provide practice looking up an opinion.
• Acquaint you with the various parts of the opinion.
• Introduce you to using *The Bluebook: A Uniform System of Citation* to cite cases.

CITATION:

♦ For purposes of Assignment One, assume you are drafting a legal document and citing the cases in citations and not in textual sentences. Consequently, follow the typeface conventions in Bluepages B2.

♦ Use Bluebook Rule 10 to cite cases. Follow the abbreviation rules in 10.2.2 and refer to table T6. Tables T1 and T10 will also be useful. Unless specifically instructed to do so, do not include information as to prior or subsequent history or weight of authority.

♦ Even if you are not instructed to give the complete cite in proper *Bluebook* format, use *Bluebook* abbreviations in your answers.

SOURCES:

Print

Official version used to write the questions:
United States Reports

Unofficial versions that can also be used to answer the questions:
West's Supreme Court Reporter
United States Supreme Court Reports, Lawyers' Edition

Online   Other Sources

WestlawNext   *Bloomberg Law*
Lexis Advance   *Google Scholar* (Filter to case law)

EXAMPLE EXERCISE:

Look up the opinion citation provided and answer the questions.

Opinion at page 291 of volume 446 of the *United States Reports*

1. Using the correct name of the opinion, cite the opinion in proper
    Bluebook citation form.
    Rhode Island v. Innis, 446 U.S. 291 (1980).

2. Which party is the respondent?
    Innis

3. What is the docket number?
    No. 78-1076

4. What is the date of decision?
    May 12, 1980

5. What is the name of the justice who wrote the opinion of the court?
    Justice Stewart

6. Who wrote the first dissenting opinion?
    Justice Marshall

7. What is the court's decision?
    Vacated and remanded

Exercise A

Look up the opinion citation provided and answer the questions.

Opinion at page 553 of volume 431 of the *United States Reports*

1. Using the correct name of the opinion, cite the opinion in proper *Bluebook* citation form.

2. Which party is the petitioner?

3. What is the docket number?

4. What is the date of decision?

5. What is the name of the justice who delivered the opinion of the court?

6. Who wrote the dissenting opinion?

7. What is the court's decision?

Exercise B

Look up the opinion citation provided and answer the questions.

Opinion at page 254 of volume 474 of the *United States Reports*

1. Using the correct name of the opinion, cite the opinion in proper *Bluebook* citation form.

2. Which party is the petitioner?

3. What is the docket number?

4. What is the date of decision?

5. What is the name of the justice who delivered the opinion of the court?

6. Who wrote the concurring opinion?

7. What is the court's decision?

Exercise C

Look up the opinion citation provided and answer the questions.

Opinion at page 83 of volume 525 of the *United States Reports*

1. Using the correct name of the opinion, cite the opinion in proper *Bluebook* citation form.

2. Which party is the petitioner?

3. What is the docket number?

4. What is the date of decision?

5. What is the name of the justice who delivered the opinion of the court?

6. Who wrote the first concurring opinion?

7. What is the court's decision?

Exercise D

Look up the opinion citation provided and answer the questions.

Opinion at page 517 of volume 510 of the *United States Reports*

1. Using the correct name of the opinion, cite the opinion in proper *Bluebook* citation form.

2. Which party is the petitioner?

3. What is the docket number?

4. What is the date of decision?

5. What is the name of the justice who delivered the opinion of the court?

6. Who wrote the concurring opinion?

7. What is the court's decision?

Exercise E

Look up the opinion citation provided and answer the questions.

Opinion at page 323 of volume 418 of the *United States Reports*

1. Using the correct name of the opinion, cite the opinion in proper *Bluebook* citation form.

2. Which party is the respondent?

3. What is the docket number?

4. What is the date of decision?

5. What is the name of the justice who delivered the opinion of the court?

6. Who wrote the concurring opinion?

7. What is the court's decision?

Exercise F

Look up the opinion citation provided and answer the questions.

Opinion at page 322 of volume 439 of the *United States Reports*

1. Using the correct name of the opinion, cite the opinion in proper *Bluebook* citation form.

2. Which party is the respondent?

3. What is the docket number?

4. What is the date of decision?

5. What is the name of the justice who delivered the opinion of the court?

6. Who wrote the dissenting opinion?

7. What is the court's decision?

Assignment Two
Chapter 5
FEDERAL COURT REPORTS

GOALS:
· Provide practice looking up and citing federal opinions.
· Use commercial reporters (*West's Supreme Court Reporter* and *United States Supreme Court Reports, Lawyers' Edition*) to cite to the official reports (*United States Reports*) when you to not have access to the *United States Reports* since *Bluebook* rules require citation to the official reports.

CITATION:

♦For purposes of Assignment Two, assume you are drafting a legal document and citing the cases in citations and not in textual sentences. Consequently, follow the typeface conventions in Bluepages B2.

♦Use Bluebook Rule 10 to cite cases. Follow the abbreviation rules in 10.2.2 and refer to table T6. Tables T1 and T10 will also be useful. Unless specifically instructed to do so, do not include information as to prior or subsequent history or weight of authority.

♦Even if you are not instructed to give the complete cite in proper *Bluebook* format, use *Bluebook* abbreviations in your answers.

Tip: For help with citing a United States Supreme Court decision in a nominative report, particularly the correct year of the decision, see http://www.supremecourt.gov/opinions/datesofdecisions.pdf.

SOURCES:

<u>Print</u>

United States Reports
West's Supreme Court Reporter
United States Supreme Court Reports, Lawyers' Edition, Second Series
Federal Reporter, Third Series
Federal Supplement, Second Series

<u>Online</u>

WestlawNext
Lexis Advance

Other Sources:

Bloomberg Law
Google Scholar (Filter to case law)

EXAMPLE EXERCISE:

For Questions 1-6, look up the opinions and answer the questions.

1. Opinion at page 76 of volume 76 of *United States Reports*

   a. Cite the opinion in proper *Bluebook* citation form. See *Bluebook* Rule 10.5 for the year.
      Smith v. Morse, 76 U.S. (9 Wall.) 76 (1870).

   b. Who was the attorney for the plaintiff in error?
      R.H. Huntley

2. Opinion at page 1 of volume 461 of *United States Reports*

   a. Cite the opinion in proper *Bluebook* citation form.
      Morris v. Slappy, 461 U.S. 1 (1983).

   b. Read the syllabus. Which constitutional amendment, clause, or privilege was at issue?
      Sixth Amendment Right to Counsel

3. Opinion at page 608 of volume 103 of *West's Supreme Court Reporter*

   a. Cite the opinion in proper *Bluebook* citation form.
      Pillsbury Co. v. Conboy, 459 U.S. 248 (1983).

   b. What is the parallel cite to the West reporter?
      103 S. Ct. 608

4. Opinion at page 547 of volume 75 of *United States Supreme Court Reports, Lawyers' Edition*, Second Series

   a. Cite the opinion in proper *Bluebook* citation form.
      Anderson v. Celebrezze, 460 U.S. 780 (1983).

   b. What is the parallel cite to the *Lawyers' Edition*?
      75 L. Ed. 2d 547

5. Opinion at page 609 of volume 337 of the *Federal Reporter*, Third Series

   a. Cite the opinion in proper *Bluebook* citation form.
      Roberts v. Carter, 337 F.3d 609 (6th Cir. 2003).

   b. Would this case be binding precedent in the Ninth Circuit?
      No

6. Opinion at page 635 of volume 746 of the *Federal Supplement*, Second Series

    a. Cite the opinion in proper *Bluebook* citation form.
        Webster v. Potter, 746 F. Supp. 2d 635 (S.D.N.Y. 2010).

    b. Is this case binding precedent in a Northern District of New York court?
        No

For Questions 7-10, follow the instructions provided in each question.

7. Your library only subscribes to *West's Supreme Court Reporter*. You know that *Bluebook* Rule 10.3.1 and table T1.1 indicate you must cite to the *United States Reports* if the case has been published in that reporter. The case you want to use is **107 S. Ct. 1756**. Look up the opinion in *West's Supreme Court Reporter*. What is its *United States Reports* cite?
    481 U.S. 279

8. You want to cite to the first sentence on page 1764 of the *West's Supreme Court Reporter* from Question 7: "McCleskey next filed a petition for a writ of habeas corpus in the Federal District Court for the Northern District of Georgia." On what page of the *United States Reports* is this sentence found? Use the star paging feature to find the answer.
    Page 286

9. Your library only subscribes to the *United States Supreme Court Reports, Lawyers' Edition*. You know that *Bluebook* Rule 10.3.1 and table T1.1 indicate you must cite to the *United States Reports* if the case has been published in that reporter. The case you want to use is **138 L. Ed. 2d 108**. Look up the opinion in *United States Supreme Court Reports, Lawyers' Edition*. What is its *United States Reports* cite?
    520 U.S. 911

10. You want to cite the first sentence on page 114 of the *United States Supreme Court Reports, Lawyers' Edition* from Question 9: "The State Supreme Court entered an order dismissing the appeal." On what page of the *United States Reports* is this sentence found? Use the star paging feature to find the answer.
    Page 914

Exercise A

For Questions 1-6, look up the opinions and answer the questions.

1. Opinion at page 91 of volume 85 of *United States Reports*

   a. Cite the opinion in proper *Bluebook* citation form. See *Bluebook* Rule 10.5 for the year.

   b. Who was the first listed attorney for the plaintiff in error?

2. Opinion at page 89 of volume 380 of *United States Reports*

   a. Cite the opinion in proper *Bluebook* citation form.

   b. Read the syllabus. Which constitutional amendment, clause, or privilege was at issue?

3. Opinion at page 1684 of volume 103 of *West's Supreme Court Reporter*

   a. Cite the opinion in proper *Bluebook* citation form.

   b. What is the parallel cite to the West reporter?

4. Opinion at page 579 of volume 58 of *United States Supreme Court Reports, Lawyers' Edition*, Second Series

   a. Cite the opinion in proper *Bluebook* citation form.

   b. What is the parallel cite to the *Lawyers' Edition*?

5. Opinion at page 922 of volume 185 of the *Federal Reporter*, Third Series

   a. Cite the opinion in proper *Bluebook* citation form.

   b. Would this case be binding precedent in the Fifth Circuit?

6. Opinion at page 718 of volume 164 of the *Federal Supplement*, Second Series

   a. Cite the opinion in proper *Bluebook* citation form.

   b. Is this case binding precedent in a Northern District of New York court?

For questions 7-10, follow the instructions provided in each question.

7. Your library only subscribes to *West's Supreme Court Reporter*. You know that *Bluebook* Rule 10.3.1 and table T1.1 indicate you must cite to the *United States Reports* if the case has been published in that reporter. The case you want to use is **125 S. Ct. 400**. Look up the opinion in *West's Supreme Court Reporter*. What is its *United States Reports* cite?

8. You want to cite to the first sentence on page 404 of the *West's Supreme Court Reporter* from Question 7: "On direct appeal, petitioner argued that our holding in *Penry I* rendered his jury instructions unconstitutional because the special issues did not allow the jury to give effect to his mitigation evidence." On what page of the *United States Reports* is this sentence found? Use the star paging feature to find the answer.

9. Your library only subscribes to the *United States Supreme Court Reports, Lawyers' Edition*. You know that *Bluebook* Rule 10.3.1 and table T1.1 indicate you must cite to the *United States Reports* if the case has been published in that reporter. The case you want to use is **150 L. Ed. 2d 198**. Look up the opinion in *United States Supreme Court Reports, Lawyers' Edition*. What is its *United States Reports* cite?

10. You want to cite the first sentence on page 203 of the *United States Supreme Court Reports, Lawyers' Edition* from Question 9: "Petitioner, Cedric Kushner Promotions, Ltd., is a corporation that promotes boxing matches." On what page of the *United States Reports* is this sentence found? Use the star paging feature to find the answer.

Exercise B

For questions 1-6, look up the opinions and answer the questions.

1. Opinion at page 306 of volume 15 of *United States Reports*

    a. Cite the opinion in proper *Bluebook* citation form. See *Bluebook* Rule 10.5 for the year.

    b. Who was the attorney for the plaintiffs in error?

2. Opinion at page 199 of volume 430 of *United States Reports*

    a. Cite the opinion in proper *Bluebook* citation form.

    b. Read the syllabus. Which constitutional amendment, clause, or privilege was at issue?

3. Opinion at page 534 of volume 81 of *West's Supreme Court Reporter*

    a. Cite the opinion in proper *Bluebook* citation form.

    b. What is the parallel cite to the West reporter?

4. Opinion at page 576 of volume 19 of *United States Supreme Court Reports, Lawyers' Edition*, Second Series

    a. Cite the opinion in proper *Bluebook* citation form.

    b. What is the parallel cite to the *Lawyers' Edition*?

5. Opinion at page 615 of volume 14 of the *Federal Reporter*, Third Series

    a. Cite the opinion in proper *Bluebook* citation form.

    b. Would this case be binding precedent in the Ninth Circuit?

6. Opinion at page 809 of volume 44 of the *Federal Supplement*, Second Series

    a. Cite the opinion in proper *Bluebook* citation form.

    b. Is this case binding precedent in a Northern District of New York court?

For Questions 7-10, follow the instructions provided in each question.

7. Your library only subscribes to *West's Supreme Court Reporter*. You know that *Bluebook* Rule 10.3.1 and table T1.1 indicate you must cite to the *United States Reports* if the case has been published in that reporter. The case you want to use is **109 S. Ct. 1794**. Look up the opinion in *West's Supreme Court Reporter*. What is its *United States Reports* cite?

8. You want to cite to the first complete sentence on page 1794 of the *West's Supreme Court Reporter* from Question 7: "Price Waterhouse also charges that Hopkins produced no evidence that sex stereotyping played a role in the decision to place her candidacy on hold." On what page of the *United States Reports* is this sentence found? Use the star paging feature to find the answer.

9. Your library only subscribes to the *United States Supreme Court Reports, Lawyers' Edition*. You know that *Bluebook* Rule 10.3.1 and table T1.1 indicate you must cite to the *United States Reports* if the case has been published in that reporter. The case you want to use is **129 L. Ed. 2d 666**. Look up the opinion in *United States Supreme Court Reports, Lawyers' Edition*. What is its *United States Reports* cite?

10. You want to cite the first sentence on page 674 of the *United States Supreme Court Reports, Lawyers' Edition* from Question 9: "On its face, this statute grants indigent capital defendants a mandatory right to qualified legal counsel[2] and related services '[i]n any [federal] post conviction proceeding.'" On what page of the *United States Reports* is this sentence found? Use the star paging feature to find the answer.

Exercise C

For Questions 1-6, look up the opinions and answer the questions.

1. Opinion at page 281 of volume 33 of *United States Reports*

   a. Cite the opinion in proper *Bluebook* citation form. See *Bluebook* Rule 10.5 for the year.

   b. Who was the first listed attorney for the plaintiff in error?

2. Opinion at page 455 of volume 400 of *United States Reports*

   a. Cite the opinion in proper *Bluebook* citation form.

   b. Read the syllabus. Which constitutional amendment, clause, or privilege was at issue?

3. Opinion at page 1407 of volume 112 of *West's Supreme Court Reporter*

   a. Cite the opinion in proper *Bluebook* citation form.

   b. What is the parallel cite to the West reporter?

4. Opinion at page 1 of volume 90 of *United States Supreme Court Reports, Lawyers' Edition*, Second Series

   a. Cite the opinion in proper *Bluebook* citation form.

   b. What is the parallel cite to the *Lawyers' Edition*?

5. Opinion at page 407 of volume 85 of the *Federal Reporter*, Third Series

    a. Cite the opinion in proper *Bluebook* citation form.

    b. Would this case be binding precedent in the Eleventh Circuit?

6. Opinion at page 1287 of volume 168 of the *Federal Supplement*, Second Series

    a. Cite the opinion in proper *Bluebook* citation form.

    b. Is this case binding precedent in a Northern District of New York court?

For Questions 7-10, follow the instructions provided in each question.

7. Your library only subscribes to *West's Supreme Court Reporter*. You know that *Bluebook* Rule 10.3.1 and table T1.1 indicate you must cite to the *United States Reports* if the case has been published in that reporter. The case you want to use is **107 S. Ct. 2636**. Look up the opinion in *West's Supreme Court Reporter*. What is its *United States Reports* cite?

8. You want to cite to the first sentence on page 2654 of the *West's Supreme Court Reporter* from Question 7: "In sum, if New York City's administrative scheme renders the vehicle-dismantling business closely regulated, few businesses will escape such a finding." On what page of the *United States Reports* is this sentence found? Use the star paging feature to find the answer.

9. Your library only subscribes to the *United States Supreme Court Reports, Lawyers' Edition*. You know that *Bluebook* Rule 10.3.1 and table T1.1 indicate you must cite to the *United States Reports* if the case has been published in that reporter. The case you want to use is **167 L. Ed. 2d 929**. Look up the opinion in *United States Supreme Court Reports, Lawyers' Edition*. What is its *United States Reports* cite?

10. You want to cite the first sentence on page 952 of the *United States Supreme Court Reports, Lawyers' Edition* from Question 9: "A difficulty arose, however, in that the Field Code and its progeny required a plaintiff to plead 'facts' rather than 'conclusions,' a distinction that proved far easier to say than to apply." On what page of the *United States Reports* is this sentence found? Use the star paging feature to find the answer.

Exercise D

For Questions 1-6, look up the opinions and answer the questions.

1. Opinion at page 426 of volume 62 of *United States Reports*

    a. Cite the opinion in proper *Bluebook* citation form. See *Bluebook* Rule 10.5 for the year.

    b. Who was the first attorney listed for the plaintiff in error?

2. Opinion at page 433 of volume 379 of *United States Reports*

    a. Cite the opinion in proper *Bluebook* citation form.

    b. Read the syllabus. Which constitutional amendment, clause, or privilege was at issue?

3. Opinion at page 2637 of volume 99 of *West's Supreme Court Reporter*

    a. Cite the opinion in proper *Bluebook* citation form.

    b. What is the parallel cite to the West reporter?

4. Opinion at page 415 of volume 164 of *United States Supreme Court Reports, Lawyers' Edition*, Second Series

    a. Cite the opinion in proper *Bluebook* citation form.

    b. What is the parallel cite to the *Lawyers' Edition*?

5. Opinion at page 1465 of volume 64 of the *Federal Reporter*, Third Series

   a. Cite the opinion in proper *Bluebook* citation form.

   b. Would this case be binding precedent in the Ninth Circuit?

6. Opinion at page 1057 of volume 114 of the *Federal Supplement*, Second Series

   a. Cite the opinion in proper *Bluebook* citation form.

   b. Is this case binding precedent in a Northern District of New York court?

For Questions 7-10, follow the instructions provided in each question.

7. Your library only subscribes to *West's Supreme Court Reporter*. You know that *Bluebook* Rule 10.3.1 and table T1.1 indicate you must cite to the *United States Reports* if the case has been published in that reporter. The case you want to use is **113 S. Ct. 732**. Look up the opinion in *West's Supreme Court Reporter*. What is its *United States Reports* cite?

8. You want to cite to the first sentence in the first **full** paragraph on page 736 of the *West's Supreme Court Reporter* from Question 7: "Petitioner argues that the word "try" in the first sentence imposes by implication an additional requirement on the Senate in that the proceedings must be in the nature of a judicial trial." On what page of the *United States Reports* is this sentence found? Use the star paging feature to find the answer.

9. Your library only subscribes to the *United States Supreme Court Reports, Lawyers' Edition*. You know that *Bluebook* Rule 10.3.1 and table T1.1 indicate you must cite to the *United States Reports* if the case has been published in that reporter. The case you want to use is **44 L. Ed. 2d 418**. Look up the opinion in *United States Supreme Court Reports, Lawyers' Edition*. What is its *United States Reports* cite?

10. You want to cite the first sentence on page 431 of the *United States Supreme Court Reports, Lawyers' Edition* from Question 9: "Local 100 does not suggest that its subcontracting agreement is related to any of these policies." On what page of the *United States Reports* is this sentence found? Use the star paging feature to find the answer.

Exercise E

For Questions 1-6, look up the opinions and answer the questions.

1. Opinion at page 269 of volume 18 of *United States Reports*

    a. Cite the opinion in proper *Bluebook* citation form. See *Bluebook* Rule 10.5 for the year.

    b. Who was the attorney for the appellants?

2. Opinion at page 389 of volume 515 of *United States Reports*

    a. Cite the opinion in proper *Bluebook* citation form.

    b. Read the syllabus. Which constitutional amendment, clause, or privilege was at issue?

3. Opinion at page 552 of volume 62 of *West's Supreme Court Reporter*

    a. Cite the opinion in proper *Bluebook* citation form.

    b. What is the parallel cite to the West reporter?

4. Opinion at page 632 of volume 100 of *United States Supreme Court Reports, Lawyers' Edition*, Second Series

    a. Cite the opinion in proper *Bluebook* citation form.

    b. What is the parallel cite to the *Lawyers' Edition*?

5. Opinion at page 1032 of volume 16 of the *Federal Reporter*, Third Series

    a. Cite the opinion in proper *Bluebook* citation form.

    b. Would this case be binding precedent in the Fifth Circuit?

6. Opinion at page 1242 of volume 185 of the *Federal Supplement*, Second Series

    a. Cite the opinion in proper *Bluebook* citation form.

    b. Is this case binding precedent in a Northern District of New York court?

For Questions 7-10, follow the instructions provided in each question.

7. Your library only subscribes to *West's Supreme Court Reporter*. You know that *Bluebook* Rule 10.3.1 and table T1.1 indicate you must cite to the *United States Reports* if the case has been published in that reporter. The case you want to use is **95 S. Ct. 392**. Look up the opinion in *West's Supreme Court Reporter*. What is its *United States Reports* cite?

8. You want to cite to the first sentence in the second column on page 400 of the *West's Supreme Court Reporter* from Question 7: "In short, assuming, *arguendo*, that the facially narrow language of the Clayton and Robinson-Patman Acts was intended to denote something more than the relatively restrictive flow-of-commerce concept, we think the nexus approach would be an irrational way to proceed." On what page of the *United States Reports* is this sentence found? Use the star paging feature to find the answer.

9. Your library only subscribes to the *United States Supreme Court Reports, Lawyers' Edition*. You know that *Bluebook* Rule 10.3.1 and table T1.1 indicate you must cite to the *United States Reports* if the case has been published in that reporter. The case you want to use is **10 L. Ed. 2d 215**. Look up the opinion in *United States Supreme Court Reports, Lawyers' Edition*. What is its *United States Reports* cite?

10. You want to cite the following sentence in the **last paragraph** on page 217 of the *United States Supreme Court Reports, Lawyers' Edition* from Question 9: "The crime in question was murder committed in the perpetration of a robbery." On what page of the *United States Reports* is this sentence found? Use the star paging feature to find the answer.

Exercise F

For Questions 1-6, look up the opinions and answer the questions.

1. Opinion at page 329 of volume 34 of *United States Reports*

   a. Cite the opinion in proper *Bluebook* citation form. See *Bluebook* Rule 10.5 for the year.

   b. Who was the first listed attorney for the plaintiffs in error?

2. Opinion at page 436 of volume 384 of *United States Reports*

   a. Cite the opinion in proper *Bluebook* citation form.

   b. Read the syllabus. Which constitutional amendment, clause, or privilege was at issue?

3. Opinion at page 552 of volume 25 of *West's Supreme Court Reporter*

   a. Cite the opinion in proper *Bluebook* citation form.

   b. What is the parallel cite to the West reporter?

4. Opinion at page 391 of volume 121 of *United States Supreme Court Reports, Lawyers' Edition*, Second Series

   a. Cite the opinion in proper *Bluebook* citation form.

   b. What is the parallel cite to the *Lawyers' Edition*?

5. Opinion at page 1105 of volume 25 of the *Federal Reporter*, Third Series

   a. Cite the opinion in proper *Bluebook* citation form.

   b. Would this case be binding precedent in the Ninth Circuit?

6. Opinion at page 944 of volume 287 of the *Federal Supplement*, Second Series

   a. Cite the opinion in proper *Bluebook* citation form.

   b. Is this case binding precedent in a Northern District of New York court?

For Questions 7-10, follow the instructions provided in each question.

7. Your library only subscribes to *West's Supreme Court Reporter*. You know that *Bluebook* Rule 10.3.1 and table T1.1 indicate you must cite to the *United States Reports* if the case has been published in that reporter. The case you want to use is **91 S. Ct. 633**. Look up the opinion in *West's Supreme Court Reporter*. What is its *United States Reports* cite?

8. You want to cite to the first sentence on page 636 of the *West's Supreme Court Reporter* from Question 7: "Pape sued Time for libel in the United States District Court for the Northern District of Illinois, there being diversity of citizenship." On what page of the *United States Reports* is this sentence found? Use the star paging feature to find the answer.

9. Your library only subscribes to the *United States Supreme Court Reports, Lawyers' Edition*. You know that *Bluebook* Rule 10.3.1 and table T1.1 indicate you must cite to the *United States Reports* if the case has been published in that reporter. The case you want to use is **109 L. Ed. 2d 184**. Look up the opinion in *United States Supreme Court Reports, Lawyers' Edition*. What is its *United States Reports* cite?

10. You want to cite the following sentence on page 202 of the *United States Supreme Court Reports, Lawyers' Edition* from Question 9: "The Court of Appeals for the Second Circuit thereby shifted the focus from the right to use the pre-existing work in a derivative work to a right inhering in the created derivative work itself." On what page of the *United States Reports* is this sentence found? Use the star paging feature to find the answer.

Assignment Three
Chapter 6
STATE COURT REPORTS

GOALS:
• Determine the status of official reports, unofficial reports, and "offprint" reporter for your state.
• Familiarize you with the features of a regional reporter volume.
• Examine a case from a state's court of last resort and a state's intermediary court of appeals and cite the case with and without parallel citations.
• Find parallel citations to cases.

CITATION:

♦For purposes of Assignment Three, assume you are drafting a legal document and citing the cases in citations and not in textual sentences. Consequently, follow the typeface conventions in Bluepages B2.

♦Use Bluebook Rule 10 to cite cases. Follow the abbreviation rules in 10.2.2 and refer to table T6. Tables T1 and T10 will also be useful. Unless specifically instructed to do so, do not include information as to prior or subsequent history or weight of authority.

♦Even if you are not instructed to give the complete cite in proper *Bluebook* format, use *Bluebook* abbreviations in your answers.

SOURCES:

Print

Atlantic Reporter, Second Series
North Eastern Reporter, Second Series
North Western Reporter, Second Series
Pacific Reporter, Second Series
South Eastern Reporter, Second Series
South Western Reporter, Second Series
Southern Reporter, Second Series

Online

Questions 10-21:
WestlawNext
Lexis Advance

Other Sources

Bloomberg Law
Google Scholar (Filter to case law)

Tip: *Google Scholar* is a good resource for finding parallel citations.

EXAMPLE EXERCISE:

1. Does your state have an official print reports for current opinions from your state's court of last resort? If so, what is your state's official print reports?

    Answers will depend on your state.

2. Which *National Reporter System's* regional reporter contains the current opinions from your state's court of last resort?

    Answers will depend on your state.

3. Does your state have an "offprint" reporter that reprints just your state's cases from the regional reporter? If so, what is the name of the "offprint" reporter?

    Answers will depend on your state.

Pull volume 510 of the *North Western Reporter*, Second Series and use it to answer questions 4-9.

4. Name the states whose cases are reported in the *North Western Reporter*.

    Iowa, Michigan, Minnesota, Nebraska, North Dakota, South Dakota, Wisconsin

5. At the time the volume was printed, who was the Chief Justice of the Supreme Court of Michigan?

    Michael F. Cavanagh

6. On what page of the volume does the Court of Appeals of Nebraska case *Shoemaker v. Head* begin?

    Page 408

7. Give the name of the case that construes 10 U.S.C.A. § 1451.

    Kramer v. Kramer

8. Give the complete cite in proper *Bluebook* citation form to the case that discusses "arson" and include the pinpoint cite to the page on which the court's discussion of arson begins.

    ***People v. Reeves*, 510 N.W.2d 198, 199 (Mich. App. Ct. 1993).**

9. Turn to the Key Number Digest in the volume. Give the complete cite in proper *Bluebook* citation form to the 1994 Supreme Court of North Dakota case digested under the topic DIVORCE and key number 237.

    ***Gaulrapp v. Gaulrapp*, 510 N.W.2d 620 (N.D. 1994).**

Retrieve the Supreme Court of Washington opinion reported at 850 P.2d 507. Use this case for questions 10-14.

10. Cite the opinion in proper *Bluebook* citation form.
State v. Wheaton, 850 P.2d 507 (Wash. 1993).

11. What is the docket number?
No. 59543-7

12. What is the name of the judge who wrote the opinion of the court?
Justice Brachtenbach

13. What is the court's decision?
Affirmed

14. You are including this opinion in a brief submitted to a Washington state court. Washington rules require the case citation to include both the official report and regional reporter cites. Provide the proper *Bluebook* citation form for this opinion that you are citing in your brief.
State v. Wheaton, 121 Wash.2d 347, 850 P.2d 507 (1993).

Retrieve the Appellate Court of Connecticut opinion reported at 637 A.2d 1116. Use this case for questions 15-19.

15. Cite the opinion in proper *Bluebook* citation form.
State v. Grant, 637 A.2d 1116 (Conn. App. Ct. 1994).

16. What is the name of the attorney who represented the appellant (defendant)?
John R. Williams

17. What is the name of the judge who wrote the opinion of the court?
Judge Frederick A. Freedman

18. What is the court's decision?
Affirmed

19. You are including this opinion in a brief submitted to a Connecticut state court. Connecticut rules require that the case citation in your brief's table of authorities must include both the official report and regional reporter cites. Provide the proper *Bluebook* citation form for this opinion that you are citing in your brief's table of authorities.
State v. Grant, 33 Conn. App. 647, 637 A.2d 1116 (1994).

20. Provide the parallel cite to the regional reporter for each of the following state reports citations:
   a. 9 Haw. App. 496
      850 P.2d 716

   b. 352 N.C. 570
      532 S.E.2d 797

   c. 201 Mont. 117
      652 P.2d 220

21. Provide the parallel cite to the state reports for each of the following regional reporter citations:
   a. 760 P.2d 670
      70 Haw. 46

   b. 452 S.E.2d 836
      317 S.C. 256

   c. 370 N.E.2d 345
      267 Ind. 370

Exercise A

1. Does your state have an official print reports for current opinions from your state's court of last resort? If so, what is your state's official print reports?

2. Which *National Reporter System's* regional reporter contains the current opinions from your state's court of last resort?

3. Does your state have an "offprint" reporter that reprints just your state's cases from the regional reporter? If so, what is the name of the "offprint" reporter?

Pull volume 420 of the *South Eastern Reporter*, Second Series and use it to answer questions 4-9.

4. Name the states whose cases are reported in the *South Eastern Reporter*.

5. At the time the volume was printed, who was the Chief Justice of the Supreme Court of South Carolina?

6. On what page of the volume does the Court of Appeals of Georgia case *Trust Co. Bank v. Thornton* begin?

7. Give the name of the case that construes 29 U.S.C.A. § 1140.

8. Give the complete cite in proper *Bluebook* citation form to the case that discusses what constitutes a "search" and include the pinpoint cite to the page on which the court's discussion of a search begins.

9. Turn to the Key Number Digest in the volume. Give the complete cite in proper *Bluebook* citation form to the 1992 Supreme Court of North Carolina case digested under the topic KIDNAPPING and key number 3.

Retrieve the Supreme Court of Arizona opinion reported at 664 P.2d 189. Use this case for questions 10-14.

10. Cite the opinion in proper *Bluebook* citation form.

11. What is the docket number?

12. What is the name of the judge who wrote the opinion of the court?

13. What is the court's decision?

14. You are including this opinion in a brief submitted to an Arizona state court. Arizona rules require the case citation to include both the official report and regional reporter cites. Provide the proper *Bluebook* citation form for this opinion that you are citing in your brief.

Retrieve the Court of Appeals of Nebraska opinion reported at 619 N.W.2d 78. Use this case for questions 15-19.

15. Cite the opinion in proper *Bluebook* citation form.

16. What is the name of the attorney who represented the appellant?

17. What is the name of the judge who wrote the opinion of the court?

18. What is the court's decision?

19. You are including this opinion in a brief submitted to a Nebraska state court. Nebraska rules require that the case citation in your brief's table of authorities must include both the official report and regional reporter cites. Provide the proper *Bluebook* citation form for this opinion that you are citing in your brief's table of authorities.

20. Provide the parallel cite to the regional reporter for each of the following state reports citations:

    a. 237 Ind. 308

    b. 36 Kan. App. 2d 262

    c. 289 N.C. 254

21. Provide the parallel cite to the state reports for each of the following regional reporter citations:

    a. 258 N.E.2d 874

    b. 619 S.E.2d 437

    c. 841 P.2d 515

Exercise B

1. Does your state have an official print reports for current opinions from your state's court of last resort? If so, what is your state's official print reports?

2. Which *National Reporter System's* regional reporter contains the current opinions from your state's court of last resort?

3. Does your state have an "offprint" reporter that reprints just your state's cases from the regional reporter? If so, what is the name of the "offprint" reporter?

   Pull volume 515 of the *Southern Reporter*, Second Series and use it to answer questions 4-9.

4. Name the states whose cases are reported in the *Southern Reporter*.

5. At the time the volume was printed, who was the Chief Justice of the Supreme Court of Louisiana?

6. On what page of the volume does the Court of Criminal Appeals of Alabama case *Edwards v. State* begin?

7. Give the name of the case that construes 33 U.S.C.A. § 905(b).

8. Give the complete cite in proper *Bluebook* citation form to the case that discusses what might be considered a "deadly weapon" and include the pinpoint cite to the page on which the court a knife is a deadly weapon.

9. Turn to the Key Number Digest in the volume. Give the complete cite in proper *Bluebook* citation form to the 1987 Supreme Court of Florida case digested under the topic PATENTS and key number 3.

Retrieve the Supreme Court of Arkansas opinion reported at 668 S.W.2d 536. Use this case for questions 10-14.

10. Cite the opinion in proper *Bluebook* citation form.

11. What is the docket number?

12. What is the name of the judge who wrote the opinion of the court?

13. What is the court's decision?

14. You are including this opinion in a brief submitted to an Arkansas state court. Arkansas rules require the case citation to include both the official report and regional reporter cites. Provide the proper *Bluebook* citation form for this opinion that you are citing in your brief.

Retrieve the Court of Appeals of Oregon opinion reported at 964 P.2d 1101. Use this case for questions 15-19.

15. Cite the opinion in proper *Bluebook* citation form.

16. What is the name of the attorney who represented the appellant?

17. What is the name of the judge who wrote the opinion of the court?

18. What is the court's decision?

19. You are including this opinion in a brief submitted to an Oregon state court. Oregon rules require that the case citation in your brief's table of authorities must include both the official report and regional reporter cites. Provide the proper *Bluebook* citation form for this opinion that you are citing in your brief's table of authorities.

20. Provide the parallel cite to the regional reporter for each of the following state reports citations:

    a. 70 Haw. 194

    b. 175 N.C. App. 45

    c. 267 S.C. 155

21. Provide the parallel cite to the state reports for each of the following regional reporter citations:

    a. 342 N.E.2d 622

    b. 604 S.E.2d 385

    c. 500 S.E.2d 423

Exercise C

1. Does your state have an official print reports for current opinions from your state's court of last resort? If so, what is your state's official print reports?

2. Which *National Reporter System's* regional reporter contains the current opinions from your state's court of last resort?

3. Does your state have an "offprint" reporter that reprints just your state's cases from the regional reporter? If so, what is the name of the "offprint" reporter?

   Pull volume 865 of the *Pacific Reporter*, Second Series and use it to answer questions 4-9.

4. Name the states whose cases are reported in the *Pacific Reporter*.

5. At the time the volume was printed, who was the Chief Justice of the Supreme Court of Hawaii?

6. On what page of the volume does the Supreme Court of Wyoming case *Armstrong v. Pickett* begin?

7. Give the name of the case that construes 26 U.S.C.A. § 7426.

8. Give the complete cite in proper *Bluebook* citation form to the case that defines "covenant warranty" and include the pinpoint cite to the page on which the court discusses that a covenant warranty must conform to Montana law.

9. Turn to the Key Number Digest in the volume. Give the complete cite in proper *Bluebook* citation form to the **first listed** 1993 Supreme Court of Arizona case digested under the topic HOMICIDE and key number 18(1).

Retrieve the Supreme Court of Connecticut opinion reported at 668 A.2d 367. Use this case for questions 10-14.

10. Cite the opinion in proper *Bluebook* citation form.

11. What is the docket number?

12. What is the name of the judge who wrote the opinion of the court?

13. What is the court's decision?

14. You are including this opinion in a brief submitted to a Connecticut state court. Connecticut rules require the case citation to include both the official report and regional reporter cites. Provide the proper *Bluebook* citation form for this opinion that you are citing in your brief.

Retrieve the Appellate Court of Arkansas opinion reported at 721 S.W.2d 670. Use this case for questions 15-19.

15. Cite the opinion in proper *Bluebook* citation form.

16. What is the name of the attorney who represented the appellant?

17. What is the name of the judge who wrote the opinion of the court?

18. What is the court's decision?

19. You are including this opinion in a brief submitted to an Arkansas state court. Arkansas rules require that the case citation in your brief's table of authorities must include both the official report and regional reporter cites. Provide the proper *Bluebook* citation form for this opinion that you are citing in your brief's table of authorities.

20. Provide the parallel cite to the regional reporter for each of the following state reports citations:

    a. 350 N.C. 315

    b. 258 S.C. 296

    c. 258 Kan. 848

21. Provide the parallel cite to the state reports for each of the following regional reporter citations:

    a. 977 P.2d 298

    b. 928 P.2d 103

    c. 148 N.E.2d 426

Exercise D

1. Does your state have an official print reports for current opinions from your state's court of last resort? If so, what is your state's official print reports?

2. Which *National Reporter System's* regional reporter contains the current opinions from your state's court of last resort?

3. Does your state have an "offprint" reporter that reprints just your state's cases from the regional reporter? If so, what is the name of the "offprint" reporter?

   Pull volume 461 of the *Atlantic Reporter*, Second Series and use it to answer questions 4-9.

4. Name the states whose cases are reported in the *Atlantic Reporter*.

5. At the time the volume was printed, who was the Chief Justice of the Supreme Court of New Jersey?

6. On what page of the volume does the Court of Special Appeals of Maryland case *Johnson v. Nadwodny* begin?

7. Give the name of the case that construes 33 U.S.C.A. § 933.

8. Give the complete cite in proper *Bluebook* citation form to the case that defines "conversion" and include the pinpoint cite to the page on which the court defines the word.

9. Turn to the Key Number Digest in the volume. Give the complete cite in proper *Bluebook* citation form to the 1983 Supreme Court of Rhode Island case digested under the topic TRUSTS and key number 372(3).

Retrieve the Supreme Court of Michigan opinion reported at 521 N.W.2d 786. Use this case for questions 10-14.

10. Cite the opinion in proper *Bluebook* citation form.

11. What is the docket number?

12. What is the name of the judge who wrote the opinion of the court?

13. What is the court's decision?

14. You are including this opinion in a brief submitted to a Michigan state court. Michigan rules require the case citation to include both the official report and regional reporter cites. Provide the proper *Bluebook* citation form for this opinion that you are citing in your brief.

Retrieve the Court of Appeals of Washington opinion reported at 882 P.2d 1207. Use this case for questions 15-19.

15. Cite the opinion in proper *Bluebook* citation form.

16. What is the name of the first listed attorney who represented the respondent?

17. What is the name of the judge who wrote the opinion of the court?

18. What is the court's decision?

19. You are including this opinion in a brief submitted to a Washington state court. Washington rules require that the case citation in your brief's table of authorities must include both the official report and regional reporter cites. Provide the proper *Bluebook* citation form for this opinion that you are citing in your brief's table of authorities.

20. Provide the parallel cite to the regional reporter for each of the following state reports citations:

    a. 57 Haw. 570

    b. 10 N.C. App. 382

    c. 312 S.C. 200

21. Provide the parallel cite to the state reports for each of the following regional reporter citations:

    a. 243 S.E.2d 129

    b. 98 N.E.2d 237

    c. 492 P.2d 657

Exercise E

1. Does your state have an official print reports for current opinions from your state's court of last resort? If so, what is your state's official print reports?

2. Which *National Reporter System's* regional reporter contains the current opinions from your state's court of last resort?

3. Does your state have an "offprint" reporter that reprints just your state's cases from the regional reporter? If so, what is the name of the "offprint" reporter?

Pull volume 614 of the *North Eastern Reporter*, Second Series and use it to answer questions 4-9.

4. Name the states whose cases are reported in the *North Eastern Reporter*.

5. At the time the volume was printed, who was the Chief Justice of the Supreme Court of Illinois?

6. On what page of the volume does the Appeals Court of Massachusetts case *Barrett v. Leary* begin?

7. Give the name of the case that construes 26 U.S.C.A. § 61(a).

8. Give the complete cite in proper *Bluebook* citation form to the case that discusses what "trespass" is and include the pinpoint cite to the page on which the court defines the word.

9. Turn to the Key Number Digest in the volume. Give the complete cite in proper *Bluebook* citation form to the 1993 Supreme Court of Illinois case digested under the topic DOUBLE JEOPARDY and key number 29.1.

Retrieve the Supreme Court of New Mexico opinion reported at 769 P.2d 84. Use this case for questions 10-14.

10. Cite the opinion in proper *Bluebook* citation form.

11. What is the docket number?

12. What is the name of the judge who wrote the opinion of the court?

13. What is the court's decision?

14. You are including this opinion in a brief submitted to a New Mexico state court. New Mexico rules require the case citation to include both the official report and regional reporter cites. Provide the proper *Bluebook* citation form for this opinion that you are citing in your brief.

Retrieve the Court of Appeals of Michigan opinion reported at 472 N.W.2d 32. Use this case for questions 15-19.

15. Cite the opinion in proper *Bluebook* citation form.

16. What is the name of the attorney who represented the defendant-appellant?

17. What is the name of the judge who wrote the opinion of the court?

18. What is the court's decision?

19. You are including this opinion in a brief submitted to a Michigan state court. Michigan rules require that the case citation in your brief's table of authorities must include both the official report and regional reporter cites. Provide the proper *Bluebook* citation form for this opinion that you are citing in your brief's table of authorities.

20. Provide the parallel cite to the regional reporter for each of the following state reports citations:
    a. 9 Haw. App. 56

    b. 229 Ind. 140

    c. 14 Kan. App. 2d 356

21. Provide the parallel cite to the state reports for each of the following regional reporter citations:
    a. 160 S.E.2d 194

    b. 958 P.2d 627

    c. 442 S.E.2d 53

Exercise F

1. Does your state have an official print reports for current opinions from your state's court of last resort? If so, what is your state's official print reports?

2. Which *National Reporter System's* regional reporter contains the current opinions from your state's court of last resort?

3. Does your state have an "offprint" reporter that reprints just your state's cases from the regional reporter? If so, what is the name of the "offprint" reporter?

    Pull volume 800 of the *Pacific Reporter*, Second Series and use it to answer questions 4-9.

4. Name the states whose cases are reported in the *Pacific Reporter*.

5. At the time the volume was printed, who was the Chief Justice of the Supreme Court of Alaska?

6. On what page of the volume does the Intermediate Court of Appeals of Hawaii case *Fukunaga v. Fukunaga* begin?

7. Give the name of the case that construes 18 U.S.C.A. § 1385.

8. Give the complete cite in proper *Bluebook* citation form to the case that discusses the meaning of "episode" and include the pinpoint cite to the page on which the court gives the ABA Standard 12-2.2(a) commentary's definition of the word.

9. Turn to the Key Number Digest in the volume. Give the complete cite in proper *Bluebook* citation form to the 1990 Supreme Court of Washington case digested under the topic WITNESSES and key number 206.

Retrieve the Supreme Court of Nebraska opinion reported at 377 N.W.2d 119. Use this case for questions 10-14.

10. Cite the opinion in proper *Bluebook* citation form.

11. What is the docket number?

12. What is the name of the judge who wrote the opinion of the court?

13. What is the court's decision?

14. You are including this opinion in a brief submitted to a Nebraska state court. Nebraska rules require the case citation to include both the official report and regional reporter cites. Provide the proper *Bluebook* citation form for this opinion that you are citing in your brief.

Retrieve the Court of Appeals of Michigan opinion reported at 828 N.W.2d 685. Use this case for questions 15-19.

15. Cite the opinion in proper *Bluebook* citation form.

16. What is the name of the attorney who represented the defendant?

17. What is the name of the judge who wrote the opinion of the court?

18. What is the court's decision?

19. You are including this opinion in a brief submitted to a Michigan state court. Arizona rules require that the case citation in your brief's table of authorities must include both the official report and regional reporter cites. Provide the proper *Bluebook* citation form for this opinion that you are citing in your brief's table of authorities.

20. Provide the parallel cite to the regional reporter for each of the following state reports citations:

    a. 343 N.C. 87

    b. 118 Ind. App. 676

    c. 246 Kan. 492

21. Provide the parallel cite to the state reports for each of the following regional reporter citations:

    a. 927 P.2d 1002

    b. 122 N.E.2d 466

    c. 190 S.E.2d 888

Assignment Four
Chapter 7
DIGESTS FOR COURT REPORTS

GOALS:
• Practice using the Descriptive-Word method of finding a case.
• Practice using the Analysis or Topic method of finding a case.
• Practice finding a case by name (Table of Cases method).
• Practice using a known topic and key number to find a case.

CITATION:

♦For purposes of Assignment Four, assume you are drafting a legal document and citing the cases in citations and not in textual sentences. Consequently, follow the typeface conventions in Bluepages B2.

♦Use Bluebook Rule 10 to cite cases. Follow the abbreviation rules in 10.2.2 and refer to table T6. Tables T1 and T10 will also be useful. Unless specifically instructed to do so, do not include information as to prior or subsequent history or weight of authority.

♦Even if you are not instructed to give the complete cite in proper *Bluebook* format, use *Bluebook* abbreviations in your answers.

SOURCES:

Print

Example Exercise:

Questions 1-3, 6-8:
  Texas Digest 2d
  Twelfth Decennial Digest, Part 1
Questions 4-5:
  South Western Reporter, Third Series
Question 9:
  West's Federal Practice Digest 4th
  Eleventh Decennial Digest, Part 3
Question 10:
  Federal Reporter, Third Series
Question 11:
  United States Supreme Court Digest
  West's Federal Practice Digest 4th
  West's Federal Practice Digest 5th
  Twelfth Decennial Digest, Part 1

Exercise A:

Questions 1-3, 6-8:
  Arkansas Digest
  Eleventh Decennial Digest, Part 2
Questions 4-5:
  South Western Reporter, Third Series
Question 9:
  West's Federal Practice Digest 4th
  Twelfth Decennial Digest, Part 2
Question 10:
  Federal Reporter, Third Series
Question 11:
  United States Supreme Court Digest
  West's Federal Practice Digest 4th
  Eleventh Decennial Digest, Part 3

Exercise B:

Questions 1-3:
West's Indiana Digest 2d
Eleventh Decennial Digest, Part 2
Questions 4-5:
North Eastern Reporter, Second Series
Question 6:
West's Indiana Digest 2d
Twelfth Decennial Digest, Part 1
Questions 7-8:
West's Indiana Digest 2d
Eleventh Decennial Digest, Part 1
Question 9:
West's Federal Practice Digest 4th
Twelfth Decennial Digest, Part 1
Question 10:
Federal Reporter, Third Series
Question 11:
United States Supreme Court Digest
West's Federal Practice Digest 4th
West's Federal Practice Digest 5th
Twelfth Decennial Digest, Part 1

Exercise C:

Questions 1-3, 6-8:
West's Ohio Digest
Tenth Decennial Digest, Part 2
Questions 4-5:
North Eastern Reporter, Second Series
Question 9:
West's Federal Practice Digest 4th
Eleventh Decennial Digest, Part 2
Question 10:
Federal Reporter, Third Series
Question 11:
United States Supreme Court Digest
West's Federal Practice Digest 4th
Tenth Decennial Digest, Part 2

Exercise D:

Questions 1-3:
West's Florida Digest 2d
Eleventh Decennial Digest, Part 1
Questions 4-5:
Southern Reporter, Second Series
Questions 6-8:
West's Florida Digest 2d
Eleventh Decennial Digest, Part 2
Question 9:
West's Federal Practice Digest 4th
Twelfth Decennial Digest, Part 1
Question 10:
Federal Reporter, Third Series
Question 11:
United States Supreme Court Digest
West's Federal Practice Digest 4th
Ninth Decennial Digest, Part 2

Exercise E:

Questions 1-3, 6-8:
West's New York Digest 4th
Twelfth Decennial Digest, Part 1
Questions 4-5:
North Eastern Reporter, Second Series
Question 9:
West's Federal Practice Digest 4th
Eleventh Decennial Digest, Part 3
Question 10:
Federal Reporter, Third Series
Question 11:
United States Supreme Court Digest
West's Federal Practice Digest 4th
Tenth Decennial Digest, Part 1

Exercise F:

Questions 1-3, 6-8:
  West's Missouri Digest 2d
  Tenth Decennial Digest, Part 1
Questions 4-5:
  South Western Reporter, Second Series
Question 9:
  West's Federal Practice Digest 4th
  Twelfth Decennial Digest, Part 2
Question 10:
  Federal Reporter, Third Series
Question 11:
  United States Supreme Court Digest
  West's Federal Practice Digest 4th
  Tenth Decennial Digest, Part 1

Online

All Exercises, All Questions:
WestlawNext

EXAMPLE EXERCISE:

In December 2014, the court granted Peter Kelly a divorce from Patricia Kelly and named them joint managing conservators of their eight-year-old son Kevin. The son's primary place of residence is with Mr. Kelly and Patricia Kelly has visitation rights. Mr. Kelly is concerned because Kevin's behavior becomes quite aggressive when he returns from visits with his mother and his grades are slipping. Mr. Kelly wants your advice on seeking a modification of custody. Specifically, he wants to know if he can limit Patricia's visitation with Kevin. You believe that Texas courts look at the best interests of the child in regards to a parent's possession of and access to the child. Determine if the Texas courts have used the best-interest-of-the-child standard in visitation situations. Look for Texas cases on the subject.

1. What are some of the specific words or phrases relevant to the fact situation?
   Answers may include: Child custody, visitation, best interest of the child

2. What topic and key number correspond with this subject?
   Child Custody **key number 178**

3. Provide the complete cite in proper *Bluebook* form to the 2007 Court of Appeals of Texas, Austin case that has the topic and key number from Question 2.
   ***Blackwell v. Humble*, 241 S.W.3d 707 (Tex. App. 2007).**

4. Which numbered headnote in the case from Question 3 discusses the specific subject at issue? Give the number of the headnote.
   15

5. On what page of the opinion in the West regional reporter does the discussion of the point of law in the headnote from Question 4 begin?
   Page 719

6. Find the 2007 Court of Appeals of Texas, Dallas case that has been assigned the same topic and key number from Question 2 and that provides further insight into the court's judgment as to the best interest of the child regarding visitation. Provide the complete cite in proper *Bluebook* form to this case.
   In re A.R., 236 S.W.3d 460 (Tex. App. 2007).

You continue to represent Mr. Peter Kelly, who now has sole managing conservatorship of his son Kevin. However, the court order granting him sole managing conservatorship imposed geographical restrictions on Kevin's primary residence. The court order mandates that Kevin must remain in Texas. Mr. Kelly has been offered a job in New York and wants to know if the court's restriction on residency is proper. Research whether a Texas court order can limit Kevin's geographical location. You know that the proper topic is *Child Custody*.

7. Examine the key numbers under digest topic *Child Custody*. You are looking for whether court orders regarding child custody can have geographical limitations. What is the key number under which this subject is classified?
   Key number 262

8. Provide the complete cite in proper *Bluebook* form to the 2009 Court of Appeals of Texas, Amarillo case that has the topic and key number from Question 7.
   In re A.S., 298 S.W.3d 834 (Tex. App. 2009).

New Problem: You are investigating whether your client Joe has a Title VII discrimination action against his former employer because Joe allegedly was unlawfully terminated based on disparate treatment. Joe thinks he was treated differently than his similarly situated coworkers because of his race. You need to determine how the court will determine whether Joe was treated differently from similarly situated employees because of his race. Your law partner recalls reading a case that might be relevant but does not know the citation of the case. She only knows that the 2004 case is from the United States Court of Appeals, Fifth Circuit and that the parties were Javier Perez and the Texas Department of Criminal Justice, Institutional Division.

9. Provide the complete cite in proper *Bluebook* form to the 2004 Fifth Circuit case.
Perez v. Tex. Dep't of Criminal Justice, 395 F.3d 206 (5th Cir. 2004).

Look up the case from Question 9. Note that the case's headnote 5 is one of the headnotes relevant to your research. Next, you want to know if there are any United States Supreme Court decisions on this point of law that would be binding on your fact situation.

10. What is the topic and key number of headnote 5 in the case from Question 9?
Civil Rights key number 1138

11. Find the 2010 Supreme Court of the United States decision that has been assigned the same topic and key number from Question 10 and that provides further information on what a Title VII plaintiff must demonstrate in a disparate-treatment claim. Provide the complete cite in proper *Bluebook* form to this case.
Lewis v. City of Chi., 560 U.S. 205 (2010).

Exercise A

You are representing Mr. Bob Brown. Unbeknownst to Mr. Brown, his neighbor Mr. Green entered his property and cut down several ornamental trees to use for holiday decorations. Mr. Brown would like to bring a trespass suit against Mr. Green, in which he will seek damages for the cutting and removing of his trees. Mr. Brown hired you to research the proper measure of damages that a Arkansas court may use when evaluating a trespass involving the cutting and removing of timber. Look for Arkansas cases that deal with this subject generally.

1. What are some of the specific words or phrases relevant to the fact situation?

2. What topic and key number correspond with this subject?

3. Provide the complete cite in proper *Bluebook* form to the 2001 Court of Appeals of Arkansas case that has the topic and key number from Question 2.

4. Which numbered headnote in the case from Question 3 discusses the specific subject at issue? Give the number of the headnote.

5. On what page of the opinion in the West regional reporter does the discussion of the point of law in the headnote from Question 4 begin?

6. Find a 2002 Court of Appeals of Arkansas case that has been assigned the same topic and key number from Question 2 and that provides further insight into the proper measure of damages in a tree cutting case. Provide the complete cite in proper *Bluebook* form to this case.

You continue to research the trespass issues relating to Mr. Green's cutting and removal of trees from Mr. Brown's yard. Mr. Brown would like to know if he can recover double or even treble damages. Research the grounds for double and treble damages in general. You know the proper topic is *Trespass*.

7. Examine the key numbers under digest topic *Trespass*. You are looking at the grounds, in general, for double and treble damages in trespass actions. What is the key number under which this subject is classified?

8. Provide the complete cite in proper *Bluebook* form to the 2003 Court of Appeals of Arkansas case that has the topic and key number from Question 7.

New Problem: Your client, Jeff Madison, seeks your legal advice. Last week, the police came to Madison's home with a search warrant. The warrant indicated the police had probable cause to search his residence for evidence of illegal gambling. While the officers were conducting the search, they placed Madison in the back of a patrol car parked on the street in front of his house. The police left Madison's house with very little evidence and Madison was never arrested or charged with any crime. Madison believes his detention in the squad car was a violation of his rights. You know that police must act reasonably when executing a warrant but do not recall any case law to support this fact. Your law partner remembers reading a case that might be relevant but does not know the citation of the case. He only remembers that the 2011 case is from the United States Court of Appeals, Eighth Circuit and that the parties are Stepnes and Ritschel.

9. Provide the complete cite in proper *Bluebook* form to the 2011 Eighth Circuit case.

Look up the case from Question 9. Note that the case's headnote 9 is one of the headnotes relevant to your research. Next, you want to know if there are any United States Supreme Court decisions on this point of law that would be binding on your fact situation.

10. What is the topic and key number of headnote 9 in the case from Question 9?

11. Find the 2007 Supreme Court of the United States decision that has been assigned the same topic and key number from Question 10 and that provides further information on the reasonableness of police officer's actions when executing a search warrant. Provide the complete cite in proper *Bluebook* form to this case.

Exercise B

You are representing Mr. Matt Green. Mr. Green wants to sue his neighbor Mr. Wilson for an injury sustained by Mr. Green's eight-year-old child Dennis. Unbeknownst to Mr. Wilson, Dennis's grandmother gave Dennis permission to play on a trampoline in Mr. Wilson's backyard. Unfortunately, Dennis fell off the trampoline and broke his arm. Mr. Green claims that Mr. Wilson should be liable for the injury since Mr. Wilson is the owner of the premises and the trampoline is a structure on his property that qualifies as an attractive nuisance. You know that an Indiana court will hold property owners liable if a building or structure on their property is deemed to be an attractive nuisance and a child is injured after going onto the premises. Under the attractive nuisance doctrine, if an adult gives a child permission to use the structure on the premises, is the homeowner liable for the child's injuries? Look for Indiana cases that examine when a person may be held negligent for premises liability for specific structures, such as trampolines, that could be attractive nuisances. Specifically look for the key number that covers particular cases under this subject.

1. What are some of the specific words or phrases relevant to the fact situation?

2. What topic and key number corresponds with this subject in general?

3. Provide the complete cite in proper *Bluebook* form to the 2003 Court of Appeals of Indiana case that has the topic and key number from Question 2.

4. Which numbered headnote in the case from Question 3 discusses the specific subject at issue? Give the number of the headnote.

5. On what page of the opinion in the West regional reporter does the discussion of the point of law in the headnote from Question 4 begin?

6. Find the 2008 Supreme Court of Indiana case that has been assigned the same topic and key number from Question 2 and that provides further information on Indiana courts treating a trampoline as an attractive nuisance. Provide the complete cite in proper *Bluebook* form to this case.

You continue to research Mr. Matt Green's attractive nuisance doctrine claim involving his child Dennis. Mr. Wilson claims that an Indiana recreational use statute has actually abolished the attractive nuisance doctrine for the state and consequently he could not be liable for Dennis's injuries. Research whether Indiana courts still recognize the adoption or existence of the attractive nuisance doctrine or whether the recreational use statute has abolished the doctrine. You know the proper topic is *Negligence*.

7. Examine the key numbers under digest topic *Negligence*. You are looking at whether the adopted attractive nuisance doctrine still exists or whether it was abolished by state law. What is the key number under which this subject is classified?

8. Provide the complete cite in proper *Bluebook* form to the 2000 Court of Appeals of Indiana case that has the topic and key number from Question 7.

New Problem: You are investigating whether your client, Larry, can bring a Title IX sex discrimination action against his local school district. Larry's daughter Beth is a high school cheerleader. She has been getting sexually harassed by Coach Edward, a teacher at the high school, and by some students on the high school football team. Larry claims that the school administration knew about the harassment, but did nothing to address it. You need to know if a school district can be held liable for sex discrimination under Title IX due to the harassment by Coach Edward and the students on the high school football team and the administration's lack of response to it. Your law partner recalls reading a case that might be relevant but does not know the citation of the case. She only knows that the 2008 case is from the United States Court of Appeals, Seventh Circuit and that the parties were Sondra Hansen and the Board of Trustees of Hamilton Southeastern School Corporation.

9. Provide the complete cite in proper *Bluebook* form to the 2008 Seventh Circuit case.

    Look up the case from Question 9. Note that the case's headnote 4 is one of the headnotes relevant to your research. Next, you want to know if there are any United States Supreme Court decisions on this point of law that would be binding on your fact situation.

10. What is the topic and key number of headnote 4 in the case from Question 9?

11. Find the 2009 Supreme Court of the United States decision that has been assigned the same topic and key number from Question 10 and that provides further information on whether a school district can be held liable for the response of the administration to the harassment under Title IX. Provide the complete cite in proper *Bluebook* form to this case.

Exercise C

You represent Mr. Sam Duncan in a workers' compensation claim against his employer. Mr. Duncan works as a stocker at the local hardware store. He was required to undergo a physical to keep his health insurance coverage. During the physical, he slipped off the exam table and injured his shoulder. His condition worsened and he had surgery to repair a torn rotator cuff. Mr. Duncan contends that his injury resulted from his employer's requirement to undergo a physical to keep his health insurance. In general, what factors will an Ohio court consider when determining if a causal connection exists between employment and injury in a workers' compensation claim?

1. What are some of the specific words or phrases relevant to the fact situation?

2. What topic and key number correspond with this subject?

3. Provide the complete cite in proper *Bluebook* form to the 1994 Court of Appeals of Ohio case that has the topic and key number from Question 2.

4. Which numbered headnote in the case from Question 3 discusses the specific subject at issue? Give the number of the headnote.

5. On what page of the opinion in the West regional reporter does the discussion of the point of law in the headnote from Question 4 begin?

6. Find the 1995 Court of Appeals of Ohio case that has been assigned the same topic and key number from Question 2 and that provides further insight into what factors an Ohio court will consider when determining if a causal connection exists between employment and injury in a workers' compensation claim. Provide the complete cite in proper *Bluebook* form to this case.

You continue to research Mr. Duncan's workers compensation claim against his employer. Mr. Duncan reveals that he did not give his employer notice of his injury after it occurred. Research whether giving notice of the accident or injury to an employer is a necessity required by an Ohio court in order for an employee to secure compensation. You know that the proper topic is *Workers' Compensation*.

7. Examine the key numbers under digest topic *Workers' Compensation*. You are looking at whether notice of accident or injury is a necessity in proceedings to secure compensation. What is the key number under which this subject is classified?

8. Provide the complete cite in proper *Bluebook* form to the 1993 Court of Appeals of Ohio case that has the topic and key number from Question 7.

New Problem: Your client, Mr. Denver, had docked his boat at Merchant's Wharf. While sightseeing at Merchant's Wharf, he was involved in a fight with another man, Mr. Hale, causing him injury. Mr. Hale is now suing Mr. Denver for his injuries. Since Merchant's Wharf is surrounded by navigable waters, Mr. Denver would like to know if he might have an admiralty defense against Mr. Hale's claims. You need to research what factors that a court may consider when deciding whether admiralty jurisdiction exists over Mr. Denver's torts. Your law partner recalls reading a case that might be relevant but does not know the citation of the case. He only knows that the 2002 case is from the United States Court of Appeals, Sixth Circuit out of Kentucky and that the parties were Edna Ayers and the United States of America.

9. Provide the complete cite in proper *Bluebook* form to the 2002 Sixth Circuit case out of Kentucky.

Look up the case from Question 9. Note that the case's headnote 7 is one of the headnotes relevant to your research. Next, you want to know if there are any United States Supreme Court decisions on this point of law that would be binding on your fact situation.

10. What is the topic and key number of headnote 7 in the case from Question 9?

11. Find the 1995 Supreme Court of the United States decision that has been assigned the same topic and key number from Question 10 and that provides further information on factors that courts will consider when deciding if admiralty jurisdiction will apply to Mr. Denver's tort claim. Provide the complete cite in proper *Bluebook* form to this case.

Exercise D

You represent Mrs. Eva Douglas. Mrs. Douglas was shopping at a department store in the local mall. She had some bags with purchases from other stores in the mall. She was approached by the store owner at the department store, who grabbed her arm and escorted her to the back office. The store owner accused her of shoplifting and would not let her leave until the police arrived. When the police arrived, they determined that Mrs. Douglas had not shoplifted anything and allowed her to leave. Mrs. Douglas would now like to assert a civil liability false imprisonment claim against the store owner. You know that a Florida court will hold the store owner civilly liable for false imprisonment if certain elements are established. In general, what elements must Mrs. Douglas prove to a Florida court to succeed in a civil false imprisonment claim against the store owner?

1. What are some of the specific words or phrases relevant to the fact situation?

2. What topic and key number correspond with this subject?

3. Provide the complete cite in proper *Bluebook* form to the 1997 District Court of Appeal of Florida, First District case that has the topic and key number from Question 2.

4. Several headnotes in the case from Question 3 discuss the specific subject at issue. Which numbered headnotes discuss the specific subject at issue? Give the numbers of the headnotes.

5. On what page of the opinion in the West regional reporter does the discussion of the point of law in the first headnote from Question 4 begin?

6. Find the 2003 District Court of Appeal of Florida, First District case that has been assigned the same topic and key number from Question 2 and that provides further insight into the elements that must be established for a false imprisonment claim. Provide the complete cite in proper *Bluebook* form to this case.

You continue to research Mrs. Douglas' false imprisonment claim against the store owner. Mrs. Douglas suffered great embarrassment when she had to explain the department-store incident to her family and friends. She also developed a facial twitch and has been losing sleep. Mrs. Douglas would like to know if she can be compensated for these damages. Research what elements of compensation a Florida court will consider when determining the damages in civil liability false imprisonment actions. You know that the proper topic is *False Imprisonment*.

7. Examine the key numbers under digest topic *False Imprisonment*. You are looking for the elements of compensation a court will consider when determining damages in civil liability false imprisonment actions. What is the key number under which this subject is classified?

8. Provide the complete cite in proper *Bluebook* form to the 2002 District Court of Appeal of Florida, Second District case that has the topic and key number from Question 7.

New Problem: You are investigating whether your client, Gloria, can pursue action against Customs officers and the federal government for violations of her constitutional rights. Gloria was on a flight from Colombia to Miami. When she landed in Miami, she was detained by Customs officers. After questioning and a preliminary search, the Customs officers, believing that she might be carrying drugs internally, detained Gloria and subjected her to more intrusive searching. When no drugs were found, Gloria was released. Determine what level of suspicion was needed to justify the Customs officers detaining Gloria and subjecting her to more intrusive searching. Your law partner recalls reading a case that might be relevant but does not know the citation of the case. She only knows that the 2009 case is from the United States Court of Appeals, Eleventh Circuit and that the parties were Janneral Denson and the United States of America.

9. Provide the complete cite in proper *Bluebook* form to the 2009 Eleventh Circuit case reported in the *Federal Reporter*, Third Series.

Look up the case from Question 9. Note that the case's headnote 12 is one of the headnotes relevant to your research. Next, you want to know if there are any United States Supreme Court decisions on this point of law that would be binding on your fact situation.

10. What is the topic and key number of headnote 12 in the case from Question 9?

11. Find the 1985 Supreme Court of the United States decision that has been assigned the same topic and key number from Question 10 and that provides further information on the level of suspicion needed to justify Customs officers detaining someone and subjecting them to more intrusive searching. Provide the complete cite in proper *Bluebook* form to this case.

Exercise E

Your client Jack is the owner of a parcel of real property located at 480 River Road in Albany, New York. Recently, the State condemned the property in an exercise of its power of eminent domain. Under eminent domain, the State can take property so long as it justly compensates the owner for the property. A restaurant building is located on Jack's property. The restaurant contains tables, chairs, counters, a commercial refrigerator-freezer, and a commercial-grade grill. Jack asks your advice as to whether the State must compensate him separately for the value of trade fixtures. In eminent domain cases when an entire tract or piece of property is taken, what is the measure of compensation for fixtures on the property? Look for cases from New York.

1. What are some of the specific words or phrases relevant to the fact situation?

2. What topic and key number correspond with this subject?

3. Provide the complete cite in proper *Bluebook* form to the 2008 Court of Appeals of New York case that has the topic and key number from Question 2.

4. Several headnotes in the case from Question 3 discuss the specific subject at issue. Which numbered headnotes discuss the specific subject at issue? Give the numbers of the headnotes.

5. On what page of the opinion in the West regional reporter does the discussion of the point of law in the first headnote from Question 4 begin?

6. Find the 2010 New York Supreme Court, Appellate Division, Second Department case that has been assigned the same topic and key number from Question 2 and that provides further insight into compensation for fixtures in eminent domain cases. Provide the complete cite in proper *Bluebook* form to this case.

You continue to research Jack's eminent domain problem. Jack would like to know the amount of compensation he is entitled to for the State of New York taking his property. Research what measure and amount of compensation meets the necessity of the State giving just or full compensation or indemnity. You know that the proper topic is *Eminent Domain*.

7. Examine the key numbers under digest topic *Eminent Domain*. You are looking for cases discussing the necessity of the measure of compensation in eminent domain to be just or full compensation. What is the key number under which this subject is classified?

8. Provide the complete cite in proper *Bluebook* form to the 2008 New York Supreme Court, Appellate Division, Fourth Department case that has the topic and key number from Question 7.

New Problem: You are investigating whether your client Helen has a libel or defamation action against a national magazine. Helen is a famous movie actress who lives and works in New York. She agreed to give an interview with the magazine. After the interview, the magazine wrote and published an article about her that contained numerous untruths. She feels injured by the untruths published in the article, as they damage her reputation in both the community and the movie industry. She believes that the magazine reporter acted maliciously when he wrote and published the article since Helen had denied several of the untrue statements during the interview. Since Helen is a public figure, determine what standard of evidence will be needed by the court to prove actual malice on the part of the magazine and its journalist so as to allow Helen to recover for libel or defamation. Your law partner recalls reading a case that might be relevant but does not know the citation of the case. He only knows that the 2005 case is from the United States Court of Appeals, Second Circuit and that the parties were John L. Karedes and The Ackerley Group, Inc.

9. Provide the complete cite in proper *Bluebook* form to the 2005 Second Circuit case.

Look up the case from Question 9. Note that the case's headnote 8 is one of the headnotes relevant to your research. Next, you want to know if there are any United States Supreme Court decisions on this point of law that would be binding on your fact situation.

10. What is the topic and key number of headnote 8 in the case from Question 9?

11. Find the 1991 Supreme Court of the United States decision that has been assigned the same topic and key number from Question 10 and that provides further information on the standard of evidence needed by the court to prove actual malice so as to allow a public figure to recover for libel or defamation. Provide the complete cite in proper *Bluebook* form to this case.

Exercise F

Your client, Michael was stopped driving home from a retirement party held at a local bar. The St. Louis, Missouri Police Department setup a roadblock a half mile from the bar. Apparently, there had been a number of alcohol-related traffic accidents in that area over the past nine months. The officers were acting within the roadblock's plan which had been vetted through the ranks of the police department. The plan called for stopping every other car and checking for license, registration, insurance, and whether or not the driver was under the influence of alcohol. However, there was no individualized suspicion that any of the drivers actually being pulled over had been drinking. As Michael drove home from the bar, the police stopped him at the roadblock and charged him with driving while intoxicated and driving on a revoked license. Michael maintains that the automobile roadblock violated his Fourth Amendment right to be free from unreasonable seizures. Research Missouri law to determine if automobile roadblocks setup to catch drivers committing automobile crimes or offenses are permitted.

1. What are some of the specific words or phrases relevant to the fact situation?

2. What topic and key number correspond with this subject?

3. Provide the complete cite in proper *Bluebook* form to the 1988 Missouri Court of Appeals, Western District case that has the topic and key number from Question 2. **Note to *Decennial Digest* users**: The case is the second listed 1988 Court of Appeals of Missouri case.

4. Several headnotes in the case from Question 3 discuss the specific subject at issue. Which numbered headnotes discuss the specific subject at issue? Give the numbers of the headnotes.

5. On what page of the opinion in the West regional reporter does the discussion of the point of law in the first headnote from Question 4 begin?

6. Find the 1988 Missouri Court of Appeals, Eastern District case that has been assigned the same topic and key number from Question 2 and that provides further insight into automobile roadblocks. Provide the complete cite in proper *Bluebook* form to this case.

You continue to work on Michael's automobile roadblock case. As you prepare for trial, you have questions about the weight and sufficiency of the evidence in a prosecution for driving on a revoked or suspended license. Michael knew his license had been suspended and had not tried to regain his license. Research Missouri case law regarding the weight and sufficiency of evidence needed in a prosecution of the automobile offense of driving without a license. You know that the proper topic is *Automobiles*.

7. Examine the key numbers under digest topic *Automobiles*. You are researching the weight and sufficiency of evidence when it comes to driving while a license is suspended. What is the key number under which this subject is classified?

8. Provide the complete cite in proper *Bluebook* form to the 1989 Supreme Court of Missouri case that has the topic and key number from Question 7.

New Problem: You are investigating whether your client Felix can bring a copyright infringement action against a competing television show producer. Felix's production company owns the registered copyrights to several old television shows one of which was a popular cartoon show as well as to modern remakes of these television shows that feature the same characters. Before the pilots of the old television shows were completed and copyrighted, publicity materials featuring images of the characters were published in magazines without the requisite copyright notice. Felix's competing television show producer acquired restored versions of the publicity materials and used the modified images of the characters on shirts. Felix believes that the use of these modified character is copyright infringement. Determine whether the scope of the exclusive rights in copyright extends to sufficiently distinctive characters from copyrighted cartoons and movies. Your law partner recalls reading a case that might be relevant but does not know the citation of the case. She only knows that the 2011 case is from the United States Court of Appeals, Eighth Circuit and that the parties were Warner Brothers Entertainment, Inc. and X One X Productions.

9. Provide the complete cite in proper *Bluebook* form to the 2011 Eighth Circuit case.

Look up the case from Question 9. Note that the case's headnote 18 is one of the headnotes relevant to your research. Next, you want to know if there are any United States Supreme Court decisions on this point of law that would be binding on your fact situation.

10. What is the topic and key number of headnote 18 in the case from Question 9?

11. Find the 1990 Supreme Court of the United States decision that has been assigned the same topic and key number from Question 10 and that provides further information on the scope of exclusive rights under copyright law. Provide the complete cite in proper *Bluebook* form to this case.

Assignment Five
Chapter 8
CONSTITUTIONAL LAW AND THE SUPREME COURT
OF THE UNITED STATES

GOAL:
• Introduce you to researching the Constitution of the United States of America and state constitutions.

CITATION:

♦ For purposes of Assignment Five, assume you are drafting a legal document and citing the cases in citations and not in textual sentences. Consequently, follow the typeface conventions in Bluepages B2.

♦ Use *Bluebook* Rule 11 to cite the United States federal and state constitutions. When citing cases, follow *Bluebook* Rule 10 and abbreviate case names using the rules in 10.2.2 and table T6. Tables T1, T10, and T16 will also be useful. Unless specifically instructed to do so, do not include information as to prior or subsequent history or weight of authority for cases.

♦ Even if you are not instructed to give the complete cite in proper *Bluebook* format, use *Bluebook* abbreviations in your answers.

SOURCES:

<u>Print</u>

For Questions 1-6:
The preferred source to use is the *Constitution Annotated*. When consulting the index to *Constitution Annotated*, the entries often lead to commentary regarding a particular topic. The article, section, clause, or amendment of the Constitution that relates to this commentary will be shown at the top of the page. To locate the text of the Constitution provision, earlier pages may need to be consulted.

For Questions 7-9:
You will use state constitutions.

<u>Online</u>

The Constitution of the United States of America: Analysis and Interpretation
        (commonly known as *Constitution Annotated*)
WestlawNext
Lexis Advance

EXAMPLE EXERCISE:

For Questions 1-6, you will research the Constitution of the United States.

1. While most people know that the minimum age for a Senator is 30, there is also a minimum number of years that the person must be a United States citizen. How many years must a person be a citizen of the United States before she is eligible to run for the Senate?

   9 years

2. List the applicable article, section, and clause of the Constitution that is the authority for your answer to Question 1.

   U.S. Const. art. I, § 3, cl. 3.

3. Does Congress have the power to punish a Member by expulsion or exclusion for misconduct that occurred before the Member was elected and sworn into office?

   No

4. Provide the complete cite in proper *Bluebook* form to the 1969 Supreme Court of the United States opinion that supports your answer in Question 3.

   ***Powell v. McCormack*, 395 U.S. 486 (1969).**

5. In 2008, the Supreme Court of the United States held that a provision of the 2005 statute eliminating federal habeas jurisdiction over alien detainees held at Guantanamo Bay, Cuba was unconstitutional as a violation of the Suspension Clause. What was the law?

   Detainee Treatment Act

6. Provide the complete cite in proper *Bluebook* form to the 2008 Supreme Court case that held unconstitutional the provision of the law from Question 5.
Boumediene v. Bush, 553 U.S. 723 (2008).

For Questions 7-9, you will research state constitutions.

7. In the following states, is there a constitutional provision making English the official language of the state? If so, cite the applicable constitutional provision.

   a. Alabama
   Yes. Ala. Const. art. I, § 36.01.

   b. California
   Yes. Cal. Const. art. III, § 6.

   c. Nebraska
   Yes. Neb. Const. art. I, § 27.

8. Which section of the Texas Constitution gives the Legislature the power to pass laws to punish medical malpractice?
   Tex. Const. art. XVI, § 31.

9. What is the name of the 1971 Texas case where the court discussed that the Legislature, under the authority of the provision from Question 8, had defined the practice of medicine and found a licensed dentist was engaged in the unlawful practice of medicine?
   Kelley v. Tex. State Bd. of Med. Exam'rs

Exercise A

For Questions 1-6, you will research the Constitution of the United States.

1. Does the President of the United States have the power to pardon someone convicted of a crime against the United States if it does not involve impeachment?

2. List the applicable article, section, and clause of the Constitution that is the authority for your answer to Question 1.

3. Does a bill become a law if it is presented to the President for approval and the President signs it?

4. Provide the complete cite in proper *Bluebook* form to the 1868 Supreme Court of the United States opinion that supports your answer in Question 3 (this case may be attributable to the 1867 term in some sources).

5. In 1965, the Supreme Court of the United States held that a provision of the 1962 statute authorizing the Post Office to detain material deemed "communist political propaganda" and forward it to the addressee after they were notified and requested it imposed an affirmative obligation on the addressee which abridged First Amendment rights. What was the law?

6. Provide the complete cite in proper *Bluebook* form to the 1965 Supreme Court case that held unconstitutional the provision of the law from Question 5.

For Questions 7-9, you will research state constitutions.

7. In the following states, is there a constitutional provision creating a separation or division of powers? If so, cite the applicable constitutional provision.

    a. Montana

    b. Tennessee

    c. South Carolina

8. Which section of the Pennsylvania Constitution prohibits the exercise of the power of suspending laws unless by the Legislature or by its authorization?

9. What is the name of the 2003 United States District Court for the Western District of Pennsylvania case where the court found that a township did not violate the Pennsylvania constitution by issuing enforcement notices for zoning violations?

Exercise B

For Questions 1-6, you will research the Constitution of the United States.

1. Does the Constitution require that excessive bail be set?

2. List the applicable amendment of the Constitution that is the authority for your answer to Question 1.

3. In order to merit copyright protection, a work must "promote the Progress of ... useful Arts." Is originality a requirement or condition that must be exhibited in the work for copyright protection?

4. Provide the complete cite in proper *Bluebook* form to the 1991 Supreme Court of the United States opinion that supports your answer in Question 3.

5. In 1990, the Supreme Court of the United States held that the 1989 statute that criminalized burning and certain other forms of destruction of the United States flag, violated the First Amendment. What was the law?

6. Provide the complete cite in proper *Bluebook* form to the 1990 Supreme Court case that held unconstitutional the law from Question 5.

For Questions 7-9, you will research state constitutions.

7. In the following states, are there any constitutional provisions regulating intoxicating liquors or alcoholic beverages? If so, cite the applicable constitutional provision(s).

    a. Idaho

    b. Michigan

    c. West Virginia

8. Which section of the Alaska Constitution protects the right of privacy in one's home?

9. What is the name of the 1975 Alaska case where the court discussed the personal use of marijuana in the home being covered in the right to privacy?

Exercise C

For Questions 1-6, you will research the Constitution of the United States.

1. Is it true that, unless there is testimony of two witnesses to the same overt act, or a confession in open court, no person shall be convicted of treason?

2. List the applicable article, section, and clause of the Constitution that is the authority for your answer to Question 1.

3. In regards to double jeopardy as applicable to the State, is the design or purpose of the prohibition against double jeopardy to protect individuals from being subjected to the hazards of trial and possibly getting convicted more than once for an alleged offense?

4. Provide the complete cite in proper *Bluebook* form to the 1957 Supreme Court of the United States opinion that supports your answer in Question 3.

5. In 2000, the Supreme Court of the United States held that a provision of the 1994 statute that creates a federal civil remedy for victims of gender-motivated violence exceeded congressional power under both the Commerce Clause and section 5 of the Fourteenth Amendment. What was the law?

6. Provide the complete cite in proper *Bluebook* form to the 2000 Supreme Court case that held unconstitutional the provision of the law from Question 5.

For Questions 7-9, you will research state constitutions.

7. In the following states, is there a constitutional provision allowing citizens the right to bear arms? If so, cite the applicable constitutional provision.

   a. Colorado

   b. Missouri

   c. Texas

8. Which section of the New Jersey Constitution addresses preference to veterans when appointing or promoting in the civil service?

9. What is the name of the 1964 New Jersey case where the court held that a veteran certified as eligible for a position due to a later examination should not automatically displace a nonveteran already holding eligibility status for the position on a list resulting from passing an earlier examination?

Exercise D

For Questions 1-6, you will research the Constitution of the United States.

1. Does Congress have the power to punish acts of piracy that are committed on the high seas?

2. List the applicable article, section, and clause of the Constitution that is the authority for your answer to Question 1.

3. Under the Constitution, Congress can establish punishments for the counterfeiting of United States coins. Does this counterfeiting provision prevent a state from punishing the issuance, passage, or circulation of counterfeit coins?

4. Provide the complete cite in proper *Bluebook* form to the 1847 Supreme Court of the United States opinion that supports your answer in Question 3.

5. In 1989, the Supreme Court of the United States held that a 1988 amendment to the statute imposing an outright ban on "indecent" commercial telephone messages was unconstitutional as it violated the First Amendment. What was the original law?

6. Provide the complete cite in proper *Bluebook* form to the 1989 Supreme Court case that held unconstitutional the amendment of the law from Question 5.

For Questions 7-9, you will research state constitutions.

7. In the following states, is there a constitutional provision addressing whether polygamy is prohibited in that state? If so, cite the applicable constitutional provision.

   a. Oklahoma

   b. New Mexico

   c. Utah

8. Which section of the Maryland Constitution says that no person will be imprisoned for debt?

9. What is the name of the 1970 Maryland case where the court discussed the obligation to support under a decree is not considered a debt, but a duty and is enforceable by attachment and possible imprisonment?

Exercise E

For Questions 1-6, you will research the Constitution of the United States.

1. Does Congress have the power to create a "uniform Rule of Naturalization"?

2. List the applicable article, section, and clause of the Constitution that is the authority for your answer to Question 1.

3. Under the Constitution, a fugitive from justice that flees to another state shall, on demand of the state having jurisdiction over the crime, be extradited back to that state. For the purpose of determining who is a fugitive from justice, do the words "treason, felony or other crime" embrace every act forbidden and made punishable by a law of a state?

4. Provide the complete cite in proper *Bluebook* form to the 1861 Supreme Court of the United States opinion that supports your answer in Question 3.

5. In 1943, the Supreme Court of the United States held that a provision of the 1938 statute establishing a presumption of guilt due to a prior conviction and the current possession of a firearm violated the test of due process found under the Fifth Amendment. What was the law?

6. Provide the complete cite in proper *Bluebook* form to the 1943 Supreme Court case that held unconstitutional the provision of the law from Question 5.

For Questions 7-9, you will research state constitutions.

7. In the following states, is there a constitutional provision prohibiting or allowing state lotteries? Provide the answer and the cite to the applicable constitutional provision.

    a. Wisconsin

    b. Washington

    c. Rhode Island

8. Which section of the California Constitution discusses access to navigable waters in that state?

9. What is the name of the 1976 California case where the court said a portion of a river was navigable and the plaintiffs had the right to free and unobstructed navigation on that portion of the river?

Exercise F

For Questions 1-6, you will research the Constitution of the United States.

1. Under the Constitution, does the President have the power to negotiate treaties with the advice and consent of the Senate?

2. List the applicable article, section, and clause of the Constitution that is the authority for your answer to Question 1.

3. Under the Sixth Amendment, the accused has a right to a speedy trial in criminal cases. Has the right to a speedy trial been held to be applicable to the states?

4. Provide the complete cite in proper *Bluebook* form to the 1967 Supreme Court of the United States opinion that supports your answer in Question 3.

5. In 1984, the Supreme Court of the United States held that a provision of the 1967 statute which banned noncommercial educational stations that were receiving grants from the Corporation for Public Broadcasting from participating in editorializing violated the First Amendment. What was the law?

6. Provide the complete cite in proper *Bluebook* form to the 1984 Supreme Court case that held unconstitutional the provision of the law from Question 5.

For Questions 7-9, you will research state constitutions.

7. In the following states, is there a constitutional provision for the conservation, preservation, or protection of natural resources in each state listed below? If so, cite the applicable constitutional provision.

   a. Virginia

   b. Florida

   c. Alaska

8. Which section of the Maine Constitution addresses double jeopardy for that state?

9. What is the name of the 1974 Maine case where the court explains when jeopardy actually begins or attaches?

Assignment Six
Chapter 9
FEDERAL LEGISLATION

GOALS:

• Trace a Public Law Number to its *Statutes at Large* cite and *United States Code* cite.

• Find a law by popular name and identify its Public Law Number, *Statutes at Large* cite, and codification location.

• Locate federal laws using key words.

• Find cases that interpret federal statutes.

CITATION:

♦For purposes of Assignment Six, assume you are drafting a legal document and citing the cases in citations and not in textual sentences. Consequently, follow the typeface conventions in Bluepages B2.

♦ Use *Bluebook* Rule 12 to cite statutes. Rule 12.5 will help you cite to statutes found online. When citing cases, follow *Bluebook* Rule 10 and abbreviate case names using the rules in 10.2.2 and table T6. Tables T1, T10 and T16 will also be useful. Unless specifically instructed to do so, do not include information as to prior or subsequent history or weight of authority for cases.

♦Even if you are not instructed to give the complete cite in proper *Bluebook* format, use *Bluebook* abbreviations in your answers.

SOURCES:

<u>Print</u>

United States Code (unannotated)
> Table volumes: Table III *Statutes at Large*, Popular Name Table

United States Code Annotated
> Table volumes: Table 2: *Statutes at Large*, Popular Name Table

United States Code Service
> Table volumes: *Statutes at Large*

<u>Online</u>

WestlawNext
Lexis Advance

<u>*Other Source*</u>

Bloomberg Law

EXAMPLE EXERCISE:

1. Provide the citation to the *United States Statutes at Large* for each of the following public laws:

   a. Public Law 107-97
      115 Stat. 960

   b. Public Law 93-89
      87 Stat. 297

   c. Public Law 96-47
      93 Stat. 344

2. Provide the citation to the *United States Code* for each of the following public laws:

   a. Public Law 100-84
      31 U.S.C. § 3101 nt

   b. Public Law 104-323
      16 U.S.C. § 461 nt

   c. Public Law 107-159
      25 U.S.C. § 415

3. Give the citation to the Public Law and the *Statutes at Large* for the enacting statute for the AIDS Housing Opportunity Act.
   Pub. L. No. 101-625, 104 Stat. 4375

4. Provide the citation to the *United States Code* where the AIDS Housing Opportunity Act is codified.
   Answer in *USC*: **42 U.S.C. 12901 et seq.**
   Answer in *USCA*: **42 U.S.C. §§ 12901, 12901 note, 12902 to 12912**
   Answer in *USCS*: **42 U.S.C. §§ 12901-12912**

5. Locate the federal law that answers the following question: In order for the President to award the Distinguished Flying Cross to a member of the Marine Corps, what must the individual achieve?

   Distinguish himself by heroism or extraordinary achievement while participating in an aerial flight

6. What is the complete cite in proper *Bluebook* form to the title and entire section in *United States Code, United States Code Annotated,* or the *United States Code Service* that answers Question 6?

   10 U.S.C. § 6245 (2012).
   10 U.S.C.A. § 6245 (West 2010).
   10 U.S.C.S. § 6245 (LexisNexis 1999).

7. Locate the federal law that answers the following question: Is a teacher permitted fair use of copyrighted material for certain educational purposes? If so, what is the complete cite in proper *Bluebook* form to the relevant title and entire section in *United State Code, United States Code Annotated,* or the *United States Code Service*?

   Yes. 17 U.S.C. § 107 (2012).
   17 U.S.C.A. § 107 (West 2005).
   17 U.S.C.S. § 107 (LexisNexis 2011).

8. A professor inquires if he can have a local copying service put together copies of material for his class. He wants 30% of four copyrighted books copied and sold as a bundle to students without paying any royalties. Provide the complete cite in proper *Bluebook* form to the 1994 Eastern District of Michigan case that held similar activity did not qualify as fair use of copyrighted materials under the law from Question 7.

   ***Princeton Univ. Press v. Mich. Document Servs., Inc.,* 855 F. Supp. 905 (E.D. Mich. 1994).**

Exercise A

1. Provide the citation to the *United States Statutes at Large* for each of the following public laws:

    a. Public Law 88-584

    b. Public Law 93-315

    c. Public Law 103-228

2. Provide the citation to the *United States Code* for each of the following public laws:

    a. Public Law 101-622

    b. Public Law 111-47

    c. Public Law 89-281

3. Give the citation to the Public Law and the *Statutes at Large* for the enacting statute for the Padre Island National Seashore Act.

4. Provide the citation to the *United States Code* where the Padre Island National Seashore Act is codified.

5. Locate the federal law that answers the following question: When can the Coast Guard render aid, saving life and property, on or under the high seas?

6. What is the complete cite in proper *Bluebook* form to the title and entire section in *United States Code, United States Code Annotated,* or the *United States Code Service* that answers Question 6?

7. Locate the federal law or laws that answer the following question: Is a criminal penalty possible for broadcasting an obscenity or using abusive or offensive language on the radio? If so, what is the complete cite in proper *Bluebook* form to the relevant title and entire section in *United State Code, United States Code Annotated,* or the *United States Code Service?*

8. Your brother-in-law, known for his socially questionable language, has purchased a citizens' band radio and has been making nightly stream-of-consciousness broadcasts. You are curious if the prosecution would have to prove that his profane language crossed state borders and was then part of interstate commerce in order to get a conviction under the statute from Question 7. Provide the complete cite in proper *Bluebook* form to the 1966 Ninth Circuit case that discusses this issue.

Exercise B

1. Provide the citation to the *United States Statutes at Large* for each of the following public laws:

    a. Public Law 100-686

    b. Public Law 99-655

    c. Public Law 85-178

2. Provide the citation to the *United States Code* for each of the following public laws:

    a. Public Law 107-51

    b. Public Law 89-68

    c. Public Law 104-279

3. Give the citation to the Public Law and the *Statutes at Large* for the enacting statute for the Fluid Milk Promotion Act of 1990.

4. Provide the citation to the *United States Code* where the Fluid Milk Promotion Act of 1990 is codified.

5. Locate the federal law that answers the following question: Who has the authority to deploy Federal air marshals on passenger aircraft?

6. What is the complete cite in proper *Bluebook* form to the title and entire section in *United States Code, United States Code Annotated*, or the *United States Code Service* that answers Question 6?

7. Locate the federal law that answers the following question: Is it a federal crime to misuse a passport? If so, what is the complete cite in proper *Bluebook* form to the relevant title and entire section in *United State Code, United States Code Annotated*, or the *United States Code Service*?

8. A diplomat wants to know if he can use his diplomatic passport to travel abroad although not part of his diplomatic assignment. Provide the complete cite in proper *Bluebook* form to the 1984 Ninth Circuit case where an indictment charged a diplomat with a violation under the law from Question 7.

Exercise C

1. Provide the citation to the *United States Statutes at Large* for each of the following public laws:

    a. Public Law 90-106

    b. Public Law 110-347

    c. Public Law 101-634

2. Provide the citation to the *United States Code* for each of the following public laws:

    a. Public Law 109-115

    b. Public Law 92-511

    c. Public Law 100-14

3. Give the citation to the Public Law and the *Statutes at Large* for the enacting statute for the Head Start Transition Project Act.

4. Provide the citation to the *United States Code* where the Head Start Transition Project Act is codified.

5. Locate the federal law that answers the following question: It is unlawful for any person to knowingly procure any human organ for valuable consideration for use in human transplantation if the transfer affects interstate commerce. What are the fines and penalties for violating subsection (a) of this law?

6. What is the complete cite in proper *Bluebook* form to the title and entire section in *United States Code, United States Code Annotated*, or the *United States Code Service* that answers Question 6?

7. Locate the federal law that answers the following question: Is an attorney paid fees from a bankruptcy client required to file a statement of the fees with the court? If so, what is the complete cite in proper *Bluebook* form to the relevant title and entire section in *United State Code, United States Code Annotated*, or the *United States Code Service*?

8. Your bankruptcy client wants to pay you a significant amount of money so that it will not go to his creditors. Provide the complete cite in proper *Bluebook* form to the 1985 Southern District of Florida Bankruptcy case that indicates the purpose of the law from Question 7 is to allow creditors to find and seek return of these excessive payments.

Exercise D

1. Provide the citation to the *United States Statutes at Large* for each of the following public laws:

   a. Public Law 93-407

   b. Public Law 108-139

   c. Public Law 106-82

2. Provide the citation to the *United States Code* for each of the following public laws:

   a. Public Law 102-46

   b. Public Law 87-785

   c. Public Law 112-4

3. Give the citation to the Public Law and the *Statutes at Large* for the enacting statute for the International Coffee Agreement Act of 1965.

4. Provide the citation to the *United States Code* where the International Coffee Agreement Act of 1965 is codified.

5. Locate the federal law that answers the following question: While the flag is being hoisted or passing in a parade, what is the proper conduct for members of the Armed Forces and veterans who are present but not in uniform?

6. What is the complete cite in proper *Bluebook* form to the title and entire section in *United States Code, United States Code Annotated*, or the *United States Code Service* that answers Question 6?

7. Locate the federal law that answers the following question: Can a veteran obtain peacetime disability compensation for a disability from personal injury suffered in the line of duty while active duty during other than a period of war? If so, what is the complete cite in proper *Bluebook* form to the relevant title and entire section in *United State Code, United States Code Annotated*, or the *United States Code Service*?

8. Your client, a military veteran, wants to know if she can receive disability benefits since she is suffering from presbyopia, a refractive error of the eye that was not caused by trauma. Provide the complete cite in proper *Bluebook* form to the 2003 Federal Circuit case that concluded presbyopia caused by aging was not a compensable disease with service connection under the law from Question 7.

Exercise E

1. Provide the citation to the *United States Statutes at Large* for each of the following public laws:

    a. Public Law 101-587

    b. Public Law 110-249

    c. Public Law 85-478

2. Provide the citation to the *United States Code* for each of the following public laws:

    a. Public Law 107-52

    b. Public Law 91-164

    c. Public Law 103-75

3. Give the citation to the Public Law and the *Statutes at Large* for the enacting statute for the Little River Canyon National Reserve Act of 1992.

4. Provide the citation to the *United States Code* where the Little River Canyon National Reserve Act of 1992 is codified.

5. Locate the federal law that answers the following question: What are the fines and/or penalties for not properly labeling cigarettes, thus violating the provisions of the cigarette labeling chapter?

6. What is the complete cite in proper *Bluebook* form to the title and entire section in *United States Code, United States Code Annotated*, or the *United States Code Service* that answers Question 6?

7. Locate the federal law that answers the following question: Does the alien-applicant applying for asylum have the burden of proof to establish he is a refugee? If so, what is the complete cite in proper *Bluebook* form to the relevant title and entire section in *United State Code, United States Code Annotated*, or the *United States Code Service*?

8. Your client is seeking asylum in the United States. Apparently even if your client meets the grounds for eligibility for asylum, the Attorney General can still deny asylum since the administrative power to grant and deny is solely with the Attorney General. Provide the complete cite in proper *Bluebook* form to the 2004 Seventh Circuit case that explains the Attorney General's authority under the law from Question 7.

Exercise F

1. Provide the citation to the *United States Statutes at Large* for each of the following public laws:

   a. Public Law 97-197

   b. Public Law 103-422

   c. Public Law 112-60

2. Provide the citation to the *United States Code* for each of the following public laws:

   a. Public Law 99-439

   b. Public Law 85-282

   c. Public Law 107-3

3. Give the citation to the Public Law and the *Statutes at Large* for the enacting statute for the Shark Finning Prohibition Act.

4. Provide the citation to the *United States Code* where the Shark Finning Prohibition Act is codified.

5. Locate the federal law that answers the following question: A flight attendant aboard an aircraft must hold a certificate of proficiency. Who issues this certificate?

6. What is the complete cite in proper *Bluebook* form to the title and entire section in *United States Code, United States Code Annotated,* or the *United States Code Service* that answers Question 6?

7. Locate the federal law that answers the following question: Are specific brands, marks, or labels required on containers of imported compressed gas brought into the United States through customs? If so, what is the complete cite in proper *Bluebook* form to the relevant title and entire section in *United State Code, United States Code Annotated,* or the *United States Code Service?*

8. Your professor asked you to research the purpose of requiring the origin of country to be marked on most imports. Provide the complete cite in proper *Bluebook* form to the 1972 United States Customs Court case that indicates Congress enacted the law from Question 7 in part so consumers could elect to buy or not buy products from that country.

Assignment Seven
Chapter 10
FEDERAL LEGISLATIVE HISTORIES
AND LEGISLATIVE MATERIALS

GOAL:

• Familiarize you with locating legislative history documents.

CITATION:

♦For purposes of Assignment Seven, assume you are citing the legislative documents in citations in a legal document, and not in textual sentences. Consequently, follow the typeface conventions in Bluepages B2.

♦ Use *Bluebook* Rule 13 to cite legislative documents. Refer to table T9 for abbreviations typically used in legislative documents.

♦Even if you are not instructed to give the complete cite in proper *Bluebook* format, use *Bluebook* abbreviations in your answers.

SOURCES:

Although a variety of sources can be used to answer the assignment questions, we recommend two free websites: Congress.gov [http://congress.gov] and GPO's Federal Digital System (FDsys) [http://www.gpo.gov/fdsys].

Use Congress.gov for Questions 1-7.

Congress.gov is a free website maintained by the Library of Congress and is the official website for U.S. federal legislative information. The site includes access to federal legislative documents, including bills, bill status, resolutions, committee reports, and the *Congressional Record*, as well as nominations and treaty documents.

Use FDsys for Questions 8-15.

FDsys is also a free website that provides online versions of official federal government publications, including the *Congressional Record*, *Code of Federal Regulations* (CFR), *Federal Register*, and the *Compilation of Presidential Documents*. Congressional documents, hearings, and reports are available, as well as public and private laws.

EXAMPLE EXERCISE:

You are tasked with conducting the legislative history for the federal statute known as the Y2K Act which was enacted in 1999 by public law 106-37.

1. Cite the public law in proper *Bluebook* format.
     Pub. L. No. 106-37

2. What is the cite to the House of Representatives bill that became the Y2K Act?
     H.R. 775

3. Who was the sponsor of the bill from Question 2?
     Rep. Tom Davis

4. What House committees considered the bill from Question 2?
     Commerce; Small Business; Judiciary

5. Give the cite in proper *Bluebook* format to the House Judiciary Committee's report on the bill from Question 2.
     H.R. Rep. No. 106-131 (1999).

6. Give the cite in proper *Bluebook* format to the conference report on the bill from Question 2.
     H.R. Rep. No. 106-212 (1999) (Conf. Rep.).

7. Look at the Actions for this bill. As recorded in the July 1, 1999 *Congressional Record*, what was the Yea-Nay vote by the Senate on the conference report for the bill from Question 2?
     Yea-Nay 81-18

     Answer location:
     Tab: Actions. Major Actions. 07/01/1999

You must now research the legislative history for the Water Resources Development Act of 1999 whose public law is 106-53.

8. Cite the public law in proper *Bluebook* format.
     Pub. L. No. 106-53

9. What is its *Statutes at Large* cite?
     113 Stat. 269

10. What is the cite to the Senate bill that became this law?

S. 507

11. Conduct a search for the bill from Question 10. Narrow your search to Date Published 1999. Look for the bill as introduced indicated by (IS). Who introduced the bill from Question 10 in the Senate on behalf of himself and others?

Mr. Warner

12. To which Senate committee was the bill from Question 10 referred?

Environment and Public Works

13. Narrow your search to Collection: Congressional Reports. Give the cite in proper *Bluebook* format to the March 23, 1999 Senate report on the bill from Question 10.

S. Rep. No. 106-34 (1999).

14. Change your Collection filter to Compilation of Presidential Documents. Find and read the President's statement upon signing the Water Resources Development Act of 1999 into law. Was President Clinton completely satisfied with all of the provisions of the bill he was signing into law?

No, he had serious reservations about the bill.

Answer location: 35 *Weekly Compilation of Presidential Documents* **1645**

15. Change your Collection filter to Congressional Record. As recorded in the July 22, 1999 *Congressional Record*, which Senate member requested a conference with the House as to the bill from Question 10?

Mr. Specter

Answer location:
145 Cong. Rec. S9112-S9113 (daily ed. July 22, 1999).

Exercise A

You are tasked with conducting the legislative history for the federal statute known as the District of Columbia Appropriations Act, 2002 which was enacted by public law 107-96.

1. Cite the public law in proper *Bluebook* format.

2. What is the cite to the House of Representatives bill that became the District of Columbia Appropriations Act, 2002?

3. Who was the sponsor of the bill from Question 2?

4. What House committee considered the bill from Question 2?

5. Give the cite in proper *Bluebook* format to the House Appropriations Committee's report on the bill from Question 2.

6. Give the cite in proper *Bluebook* format to the conference report on the bill from Question 2.

7. Look at the Actions for this bill. As recorded in the December 6, 2001 *Congressional Record*, on agreeing to the conference report, what were the Yeas and Nays by the House on the conference report for the bill from Question 2?

You must now research the legislative history for the Detroit River International Wildlife Refuge Establishment Act which was enacted in 2001 by public law 107-91.

8. Cite the public law in proper *Bluebook* format.

9. What is its *Statutes at Large* cite?

10. What is the cite to the House bill that became this law?

11. Conduct a search for the bill from Question 10. Narrow your search to Date Published 2001. Look for the bill as introduced indicated by (IH). Who introduced the bill from Question 10 in the House?

12. To which House committee was the bill from Question 10 referred?

13. Narrow your search to Collection: Congressional Reports. Give the cite in proper *Bluebook* format to the November 5, 2001 House report on the bill from Question 10.

14. Change your Collection filter to Compilation of Presidential Documents. Find and read the President's statement upon signing the Detroit River International Wildlife Refuge Establishment Act into law. How many diving ducks does President Bush say stop in the River to rest and feed during their fall migration?

15. Change your Collection filter to Congressional Record. As recorded in the November 27, 2001 *Congressional Record*, about the bill from Question 10, which House member says "[s]adly, up to 95 percent of the original wetlands of the Detroit River have been lost to development"?

Exercise B

You are tasked with conducting the legislative history for the federal statute known as the **Keeping Children and Families Safe Act of 2003 enacted by public law 108-36.**

1. Cite the public law in proper *Bluebook* format.

2. What is the cite to the Senate bill that became the Keeping Children and Families Safe Act of 2003?

3. Who was the sponsor of the bill from Question 2?

4. What Senate committee considered the bill from Question 2?

5. Give the cite in proper *Bluebook* format to the Senate Health, Education, Labor, and Pensions Committee's report on the bill from Question 2.

6. Give the cite in proper *Bluebook* format to the conference report on the bill from Question 2.

7. Look at the Actions for this bill. As recorded in the June 19, 2003 *Congressional Record*, what happened to the conference report in the Senate?

You must now research the legislative history for the **Check Clearing for the 21st Century Act which was enacted in 2003 by public law 108-100.**

8. Cite the public law in proper *Bluebook* format.

9. What is its *Statutes at Large* cite?

10. What is the cite to the House bill that became this law?

11. Conduct a search for the bill from Question 10. Narrow your search to Date Published 2003. Look for the bill as introduced indicated by (IH). Who introduced the bill from Question 10 in the House on behalf of herself and others?

12. To which House committee was the bill from Question 10 referred?

13. Narrow your search to Collection: Congressional Reports. Give the cite in proper *Bluebook* format to the June 2, 2003 House report on the bill from Question 10.

14. Change your Collection filter to Compilation of Presidential Documents. Find and read the President's statement upon signing the Check Clearing for the 21st Century Act into law. What does President Bush say this Act is intended to do?

15. Change your Collection filter to Congressional Record. As recorded in the October 15, 2003 *Congressional Record*, which Senate member said "I support the conference report to the Check Clearing for the 21st Century Act or Check 21 Act. This is an important piece of legislation and a high priority for the Federal Reserve Board[,]" when the Senate was considering the conference report to the bill from Question 10?

Exercise C

You are tasked with conducting the legislative history for the federal statute known as the **Tax Increase Prevention and Reconciliation Act of 2005** whose public law is 109-222.

1. Cite the public law in proper *Bluebook* format.

2. What is the cite to the House of Representatives bill that became the Tax Increase Prevention and Reconciliation Act of 2005?

3. Who was the sponsor of the bill from Question 2?

4. What House committee considered the bill from Question 2?

5. Give the cite in proper *Bluebook* format to the House Ways and Means Committee's report on the bill from Question 2.

6. Give the cite in proper *Bluebook* format to the conference report on the bill from Question 2.

7. Look at the Actions for this bill. As recorded in the May 11, 2006 *Congressional Record*, what was the Yea-Nay vote by the Senate on the conference report for the bill from Question 2?

You must now research the legislative history for the **Coastal Barrier Resources Reauthorization Act of 2005** whose public law is 109-226.

8. Cite the public law in proper *Bluebook* format.

9. What is its *Statutes at Large* cite?

10. What is the cite to the Senate bill that became this law?

11. Conduct a search for the bill from Question 10. Narrow your search to Date Published 2005. Look for the bill as introduced indicated by (IS). Who introduced the bill from Question 10 in the Senate on behalf of himself and others?

12. To which Senate committee was the bill from Question 10 referred?

13. Narrow your search to Collection: Congressional Reports. Give the cite in proper *Bluebook* format to the November 15, 2005 Senate report on the bill from Question 10.

14. Change your Collection filter to Compilation of Presidential Documents and the Date Published filter to 2006. Find and read the President's statement upon signing the Coastal Barrier Resources Reauthorization Act of 2005 into law. What did President Bush say this Act provides for and authorizes?

15. Change your Collection filter to Congressional Record. As recorded in the May 16, 2006 *Congressional Record*, which House member moved to suspend the rules and pass the Senate bill from Question 10 to reauthorize the Coastal Barrier Resources Act?

Exercise D

You are tasked with conducting the legislative history for the federal statute known as the **Improving Head Start for School Readiness Act of 2007 whose public law is 110-134.**

1. Cite the public law in proper *Bluebook* format.

2. What is the cite to the House of Representatives bill that became the Improving Head Start for School Readiness Act of 2007?

3. Who was the sponsor of the bill from Question 2?

4. What House committee considered the bill from Question 2?

5. Give the cite in proper *Bluebook* format to the House Education and Labor Committee's report on the bill from Question 2.

6. Give the cite in proper *Bluebook* format to the conference report on the bill from Question 2.

7. Look at the Actions for this bill. As recorded in the November 14, 2007 *Congressional Record*, what was the result of the Yea-Nay vote by the Senate on the conference report for the bill from Question 2?

You must now research the legislative history for the **United States-Peru Trade Promotion Agreement Implementation Act which was enacted in 2007 by public law 110-138.**

8. Cite the public law in proper *Bluebook* format.

9. What is its *Statutes at Large* cite?

10. What is the cite to the House bill that became this law?

11. Conduct a search for the bill from Question 10. Narrow your search to Date Published 2007. Look for the bill as introduced indicated by (IH). Who introduced the bill from Question 10 in the House on behalf of himself and another?

12. To which House committee was the bill from Question 10 referred?

13. Narrow your search to Collection: Congressional Reports. Give the cite in proper *Bluebook* format to the November 5, 2007 House report on the bill from Question 10.

14. Change your Collection filter to Compilation of Presidential Documents. Find and read the President's statement upon signing the United States-Peru Trade Promotion Agreement Implementation Act into law. What does President Bush say is the reason that members of the Cabinet have joined them for the signing of this bill?

15. Change your Collection filter to Congressional Record. As recorded in the November 8, 2007 *Congressional Record*, which House member mistakenly voted "yea" instead of "nay" as to the bill from Question 10?

Exercise E

You are tasked with conducting the legislative history for the federal statute known as the Agriculture, Rural Development, Food and Drug Administration, and Related Agencies Appropriations Act, 2010 whose public law is 111-80.

1. Cite the public law in proper *Bluebook* format.

2. What is the cite to the House of Representatives bill that became the Agriculture, Rural Development, Food and Drug Administration, and Related Agencies Appropriations Act, 2010?

3. Who was the sponsor of the bill from Question 2?

4. What House committee considered the bill from Question 2?

5. Give the cite in proper *Bluebook* format to the House Appropriations Committee's report on the bill from Question 2.

6. Give the cite in proper *Bluebook* format to the conference report on the bill from Question 2.

7. Look at the Actions for this bill. As recorded in the October 8, 2009 *Congressional Record*, when the conference report was considered in the Senate, what was reported as the total spending included in the bill?

You must now research the legislative history for the Internet Tax Nondiscrimination Act which was enacted in 2001 by public law 107-75.

8. Cite the public law in proper *Bluebook* format.

9. What is its *Statutes at Large* cite?

10. What is the cite to the House bill that became this law?

11. Conduct a search for the bill from Question 10. Narrow your search to Date Published 2001. Look for the bill as introduced indicated by (IH). Who introduced the bill from Question 10 in the House on behalf of himself and others?

12. To which House committee was the bill from Question 10 referred?

13. Narrow your search to Collection: Congressional Reports. Give the cite in proper *Bluebook* format to the October 16, 2001 House report on the bill from Question 10.

14. Change your Collection filter to Compilation of Presidential Documents. Find and read the President's statement upon signing the Internet Tax Nondiscrimination Act into law. What does President Bush say about the importance of extending the moratorium that this bill provides?

15. Change your Collection filter to Congressional Record. As recorded in the October 16, 2001 *Congressional Record*, which House member stated that "the sky is not falling" as to the bill from Question 10?

Exercise F

You are tasked with conducting the legislative history for the federal statute known as the Coast Guard and Maritime Transportation Act of 2006 whose public law is 109-241.

1. Cite the public law in proper *Bluebook* format.

2. What is the cite to the House of Representatives bill that became the Coast Guard and Maritime Transportation Act of 2006?

3. Who was the sponsor of the bill from Question 2?

4. What House committees considered the bill from Question 2?

5. Give the cite in proper *Bluebook* format to the House Transportation and Infrastructure Committee's report on the bill from Question 2.

6. Give the cite in proper *Bluebook* format to the conference report on the bill from Question 2.

7. Look at the Actions for this bill. As recorded in the April 6, 2006 *Congressional Record*, who was responsible for submitting the conference report and statement on the bill to the House?

You must now research the legislative history for the Jobs and Growth Tax Relief Reconciliation Act of 2003 whose public law is 108-27.

8. Cite the public law in proper *Bluebook* format.

9. What is its *Statutes at Large* cite?

10. What is the cite to the House bill that became this law?

11. Conduct a search for the bill from Question 10. Narrow your search to Date Published 2003. Look for the bill as introduced indicated by (IH). Who introduced the bill from Question 10 in the House?

12. To which House committee was the bill from Question 10 referred?

13. Narrow your search to Collection: Congressional Reports and Organization: Committee on Ways and Means. Give the cite in proper *Bluebook* format to the May 8, 2003 House report on the bill from Question 10.

14. Remove the Organization filter and change your Collection filter to Compilation of Presidential Documents. Find and read the President's statement upon signing the Jobs and Growth Tax Relief Reconciliation Act of 2003 into law. What commonsense economic principle does President Bush say this law reflects?

15. Change your Collection filter to Congressional Record. Change your Date Published filter to May 23, 2003 by drilling down to the specific month and day using the plus sign buttons. As recorded in the May 23, 2003 *Congressional Record*, how much time did the President pro tempore say was allotted for debate when the Senate began considering the conference report relating to the bill from Question 10?

Assignment Eight
Chapter 11
STATE AND MUNICIPAL LEGISLATION

GOALS:
· Find state statutes using key words and cite the law.
· Identify an original enacting law.
· Determine if there are any court opinions interpreting the law
· Identify cross references from the law to other laws in your state.
· Locate and cite an ordinance from your city.

CITATION:

♦For purposes of Assignment Eight, assume you are citing the statutes and cases in citations in a legal document. Consequently, follow the typeface conventions in Bluepages B2.

♦Use *Bluebook* Rule 12 to cite statutes, ordinances, and municipal codes. Review table T1 for guidance.

♦Use *Bluebook* Rule 10 to cite cases. Apply the abbreviation rules in 10.2.2 and use table T6. Tables T1 and T10 will also be useful. Unless specifically instructed to do so, do not include information as to prior or subsequent history or weight of authority.

♦Even if you are not instructed to give the complete cite in proper *Bluebook* format, use *Bluebook* abbreviations in your answers.

SOURCES:

Print

Statutes or Codes for your state
Municipal Code for your city (probably online)

Online

WestlawNext
Lexis Advance
Check for an online version of the Municipal Code for your city.

EXAMPLE EXERCISE:

1. Find your state's Safe Haven law, which gives the parameters where a parent can safely and anonymously surrender or "abandon" a child without fear of prosecution. What is the maximum age of a child that may be left at a Safe Haven? Note: For this example, our jurisdiction is Texas.

   A child who appears to be 60 days old or younger

2. Cite the law in proper *Bluebook* format.

   Tex. Fam. Code Ann. § 262.302 (West 2014).

3. Provide the cite in proper *Bluebook* format to the original law that enacted the law from Question 2. Do not include the codification information. **Note**: The date of enactment is the date of the final legislative action on the bill, not the date of executive approval.

   Act of May 20, 1999, 76th Leg., R.S. ch. 1087 § 2, 1999 Tex. Gen. Laws 3947, 3949.

4. Have any courts interpreted your law? If so, provide the cite in proper *Bluebook* format to the first listed case.

   No

5. Under your law, are there cross references to related sections of your state's statutes? If so, give the first listed cross reference.

   Tex. Penal Code Ann. § 22.041

Locate the municipal ordinances for the city in which your school is located and complete Questions 6 & 7.

6. Does your city have a ban on smoking in restaurants? If so, give the cite to the ordinance. Note: For this example, our location is Fort Worth, Texas.

   Yes. Fort Worth, Tex., Code of Ordinances § 29.5-2 (2015).

7. How current was the source you used to answer Question 6?

   Current through Ordinance 21683-03-2015, passed 3-3-2015

Exercise A

1. Find your state's laws that revoke the professional or occupational license of an individual who fails to pay child support. What is the amount of delinquency that triggers the revocation?

2. Cite the law in proper *Bluebook* format.

3. Provide the cite in proper *Bluebook* format to the original law that enacted the law from Question 2. Do not include the codification information. **Note**: The date of enactment is the date of the final legislative action on the bill, not the date of executive approval.

4. Have any courts interpreted your law? If so, provide the cite in proper *Bluebook* format to the first listed case.

5. Under your law, are there cross references to related sections of your state's statutes? If so, give the first listed cross reference.

Locate the municipal ordinances for the city in which your school is located and complete Questions 6 & 7.

6. Does your city have a ban on unreasonable noise? If so, give the cite to the ordinance.

7. How current was the source you used to answer Question 6?

Exercise B

1. Find your state's laws as to whether a debtor in bankruptcy is allowed to choose between state law exemptions and federal exemptions or whether the debtor is required to use the state exemptions. Is a bankruptcy debtor permitted to use the federal exemptions in your state?

2. Cite the law in proper *Bluebook* format.

3. Provide the cite in proper *Bluebook* format to the original law that enacted the law from Question 2. Do not include the codification information. **Note**: The date of enactment is the date of the final legislative action on the bill, not the date of executive approval.

4. Have any courts interpreted your law? If so, provide the cite in proper *Bluebook* format to the first listed case.

5. Under your law, are there cross references to related sections of your state's statutes? If so, give the first listed cross reference.

   Locate the municipal ordinances for the city in which your school is located and complete Questions 6 & 7.

6. Does your city have a ban on unrestrained dogs? If so, give the cite to the ordinance.

7. How current was the source you used to answer Question 6?

Exercise C

1. Find your state's state securities regulations, commonly referred to as "blue sky laws," dealing with the issue and sale of securities. Who may register securities in your state?

2. Cite the law in proper *Bluebook* format.

3. Provide the cite in proper *Bluebook* format to the original law that enacted the law from Question 2. Do not include the codification information. **Note**: The date of enactment is the date of the final legislative action on the bill, not the date of executive approval.

4. Have any courts interpreted your law? If so, provide the cite in proper *Bluebook* format to the first listed case.

5. Under your law, are there cross references to related sections of your state's statutes? If so, give the first listed cross reference.

Locate the municipal ordinances for the city in which your school is located and complete Questions 6 & 7.

6. Does your city have a tree ordinance? If so, give the cite to the ordinance.

7. How current was the source you used to answer Question 6?

Exercise D

1. Find your state's lemon laws, also known as new car warranty laws that protect the buyers of new motor vehicles that are always in need of repair. What is the time limit for a buyer to obtain manufacturer repair in your state?

2. Cite the law in proper *Bluebook* format.

3. Provide the cite in proper *Bluebook* format to the original law that enacted the law from Question 2. Do not include the codification information. **Note**: The date of enactment is the date of the final legislative action on the bill, not the date of executive approval.

4. Have any courts interpreted your law? If so, provide the cite in proper *Bluebook* format to the first listed case.

5. Under your law, are there cross references to related sections of your state's statutes? If so, give the first listed cross reference.

Locate the municipal ordinances for the city in which your school is located and complete Questions 6 & 7.

6. Does your city have a sign ordinance? If so, give the cite to the ordinance.

7. How current was the source you used to answer Question 6?

Exercise E

1. Find your state's law(s) that enumerate the legal holidays recognized by your state. How many legal state holidays does your state identify?

2. Cite the law in proper *Bluebook* format.

3. Provide the cite in proper *Bluebook* format to the original law that enacted the law from Question 2. Do not include the codification information. **Note**: The date of enactment is the date of the final legislative action on the bill, not the date of executive approval.

4. Have any courts interpreted your law? If so, provide the cite in proper *Bluebook* format to the first listed case.

5. Under your law, are there cross references to related sections of your state's statutes? If so, give the first listed cross reference.

   Locate the municipal ordinances for the city in which your school is located and complete Questions 6 & 7.

6. Does your city have an ordinance for alcohol permits? If so, give the cite to the ordinance.

7. How current was the source you used to answer Question 6?

Exercise F

1. Find your state's laws concerning compulsory or required education. What is the general age range where children are required to attend school in your state?

2. Cite the law in proper *Bluebook* format.

3. Provide the cite in proper *Bluebook* format to the original law that enacted the law from Question 2. Do not include the codification information.

4. Have any courts interpreted your law? If so, provide the cite in proper *Bluebook* format to the first listed case.

5. Under your law, are there cross references to related sections of your state's statutes? If so, give the first listed cross reference.

    Locate the municipal ordinances for the city in which your school is located and complete Questions 6 & 7.

6. Does your city have a parking ordinance? If so, give the cite to the ordinance.

7. How current was the source you used to answer Question 6?

GOALS:
· Familiarize you with the sources of federal court rules.
· Provide practice finding and citing federal court rules.

CITATION:

♦ For purposes of Assignment Nine, assume you are citing the law in citations in a legal document. Consequently, follow the typeface conventions in Bluepages B2.

♦ Use *Bluebook* Rule 12.9.3 to cite rules of procedure and Rule 10 to cite cases. Apply the abbreviation rules in 10.2.2 and use table T6. Tables T1 and T10 will also be useful. Unless specifically instructed to do so, do not include information as to prior or subsequent history or weight of authority.

♦Even if you are not instructed to give the complete cite in proper *Bluebook* format, use *Bluebook* abbreviations in your answers.

SOURCES:

Print

Federal Rules of Civil Procedure
  United States Code, Title 28 Appendix (unannotated)
  United States Code Annotated, Title 28 Rules volumes
  United States Code Service, Court Rules volumes

Federal Rules of Criminal Procedure
  United States Code, Title 18 Appendix (unannotated)
  United States Code Annotated, Title 18 Rules volumes
  United States Code Service, Court Rules volumes

Federal Rules of Appellate Procedure
  United States Code, Title 28 Appendix (unannotated)
  United States Code Annotated, Title 28 Rules volumes
  United States Code Service, Court Rules volumes

Online

WestlawNext

Other Sources

Lexis Advance
Bloomberg Law
LLRX.com: http://www.llrx.com/courtrules
Public Library of Law: http://www.plol.org
Legal Information Institute: http://www.law.cornell.edu

EXAMPLE EXERCISE:

1. Under Federal Rule of Civil Procedure 3, how is a civil action commenced?
   By filing a complaint with the court

2. Under the Federal Rules of Civil Procedure, may a court issue a temporary restraining order without notice to the adverse party?
   Yes

3. Cite the rule from Question 2 in proper *Bluebook* format. When citing the rule, cite to the overall rule number. It is not necessary to include the subsection.
   Fed. R. Civ. P. 65.

4. Provide the cite in proper *Bluebook* format to the 1993 United States Sixth Circuit Court of Appeals case applying the rule from Question 3 in which the court held that the applicant seeking an ex parte temporary restraining order based upon the assertion that the defendant would have ignored the court order and disposed of evidence, must show that the defendant had a history of disposing of evidence or violating court orders.
   ***First Tech. Safety Sys., Inc. v. Depinet,* 11 F.3d 641 (6th Cir. 1993).**

5. Under Federal Rule of Criminal Procedure 30, can any party request in writing that the court give the jury specific jury instructions?
   Yes

6. Under the Federal Rules of Criminal Procedure if a grand jury indicts an individual for a crime and the court issues an arrest warrant for the defendant named in the indictment, to whom must the court issue the arrest warrant?
   An officer authorized to execute the arrest warrant

7. Cite the rule from Question 6 in proper *Bluebook* format. When citing the rule, cite to the overall rule number. It is not necessary to include the subsection.
   Fed. R. Crim. P. 9.

8. Provide the cite in proper *Bluebook* format to the 1984 United States District Court for the Northern District of Ohio case applying the rule from Question 7 in which the court held that once the attorney for the government has requested an arrest warrant for an individual named in a fair and properly drawn indictment, the court must issue the arrest warrant.

   In re Sturman, 604 F. Supp. 278 (N.D. Ohio 1984).

9. Under Federal Rule of Appellate Procedure 32.1, may a court prohibit citing an unpublished federal judicial opinion issued after January 1, 2007?

   No

10. Under the Federal Rules of Appellate Procedure, must a state get consent of the parties or leave of the court to file an amicus curiae brief?

    No

11. Cite the rule from Question 10 in proper *Bluebook* format. When citing the rule, cite to the overall rule number. It is not necessary to include the subsection.

    Fed. R. App. P. 29.

12. Provide the cite in proper *Bluebook* format to the 2002 United States Third Circuit Court of Appeals case interpreting the rule from Question 11 in which the court held that the physicians who had participated in employee benefit plans were granted leave to file brief as amicus curiae on appeal.

    Neonatology Assocs. v. Comm'r , 292 F.3d 128 (3rd 2002).

Exercise A

1. Under Federal Rule of Civil Procedure 8, what must a party do if they intend in good faith to deny part of an allegation?

2. Under the Federal Rules of Civil Procedure, may a deposition be taken in a foreign country under a letter of request, whether or not it is captioned a "letter rogatory"?

3. Cite the rule from Question 2 in proper *Bluebook* format. When citing the rule, cite to the overall rule number. It is not necessary to include the subsection.

4. Provide the cite in proper *Bluebook* format to the 1996 United States District Court for the Eastern District of Oklahoma case applying the rule from Question 3 in which the court, in regards to disqualification for interest and parties, held that a party's administration of oaths in a deposition proceeding violated the rule against giving depositions before someone financially interested, including a party's relative or employee, in the action and making the depositions inadmissible.

5. Under Federal Rule of Criminal Procedure 1, what is the definition of "Judge"?

6. Under the Federal Rules of Criminal Procedure, if a defendant waives prosecution by indictment, may an offense punishable by imprisonment for more than one year be prosecuted by information?

7. Cite the rule from Question 6 in proper *Bluebook* format. When citing the rule, cite to the overall rule number. It is not necessary to include the subsection.

8. Provide the cite in proper *Bluebook* format to the 1996 United States Fifth Circuit Court of Appeals case applying the rule from Question 7 in which the court, in regards to guilty pleas and the waiver of the right to indictment, held that with his guilty plea, the defendant waived prosecution by indictment and his waiver of his right to indictment satisfied the rule allowing the felony to be prosecuted by information if he waives prosecution by indictment.

9. Under Federal Rule of Appellate Procedure 1, does "state" include any United States commonwealth or territory?

10. Under the Federal Rules of Appellate Procedure, when an appeal is within the court of appeal's discretion, to request permission to appeal, must a party file a petition for permission to appeal?

11. Cite the rule from Question 10 in proper *Bluebook* format. When citing the rule, cite to the overall rule number. It is not necessary to include the subsection.

12. Provide the cite in proper *Bluebook* format to the 1985 United States Fifth Circuit Court of Appeals case interpreting the rule from Question 11 in which the court, in regards to the necessity of petition and the timely filing of the request for permissive appeal, held that where the district court entered the requisite certificate for appealability and the plaintiff timely filed notice of appeal but did not file with the court of appeals a request for permissive appeal within the required time frame, the court of appeals lacked jurisdiction to consider granting the discretionary appeal, and it warranted a dismissal of the appeal for lack of appellate jurisdiction.

Exercise B

1. Under Federal Rule of Civil Procedure 11, under the requirements for an order, what must an order imposing a sanction describe?

2. Under the Federal Rules of Civil Procedure, what contents must an examiner include in a report relating to a mental examination?

3. Cite the rule from Question 2 in proper *Bluebook* format. When citing the rule, cite to the overall rule number. It is not necessary to include the subsection.

4. Provide the cite in proper *Bluebook* format to the 1994 United States District Court for the Northern District of Illinois case applying the rule from Question 3 in which the court, in regards to protective orders, held that an employment discrimination party's motion for a protective order against psychological testing would be allowed, where the party adduced substantial information demonstrating the inadequacy of the validity factors and the correlation factors of the psychological tests in question.

5. Under Federal Rule of Criminal Procedure 10, must an arraignment be conducted in open court?

6. Under the Federal Rules of Criminal Procedure, in regards to depositions, when the court orders one to be taken, may it require the deponent to produce at the deposition any designated material that is not privileged?

7. Cite the rule from Question 6 in proper *Bluebook* format. When citing the rule, cite to the overall rule number. It is not necessary to include the subsection.

8. Provide the cite in proper *Bluebook* format to the 1984 United States First Circuit Court of Appeals case applying the rule from Question 7 in which the court, in regards to the physical condition or incapacity of a witness and reasons for unavailability, held that the physical condition of two witnesses of advanced age which prevented them from leaving their house which was 60 miles away qualified as "exceptional circumstances" for purposes of determining the propriety of taking their videotaped depositions.

9. Under Federal Rule of Appellate Procedure 3, is an appeal from a judgment by a magistrate judge in a civil case taken in the same way as an appeal from a district court judgment?

10. Under the Federal Rules of Appellate Procedure, may a court of appeals suspend provisions of rules for good cause and order proceedings as it directs, except as otherwise may be provided in the rules?

11. Cite the rule from Question 10 in proper *Bluebook* format. When citing the rule, cite to the overall rule number. It is not necessary to include the subsection.

12. Provide the cite in proper *Bluebook* format to the 2004 United States Second Circuit Court of Appeals case interpreting the rule from Question 11 in which the court held, in regards to reinstatement of appeal or the jurisdiction of the court of appeals, that the Court of Appeals ordinarily has discretion to reinstate an appeal that was dismissed due to appellate default.

Exercise C

1. Under Federal Rule of Civil Procedure 13, what may a pleading permissively state as a counterclaim against an opposing party?

2. Under the Federal Rules of Civil Procedure, when taking testimony, may a court appoint an interpreter of its choosing?

3. Cite the rule from Question 2 in proper *Bluebook* format. When citing the rule, cite to the overall rule number. It is not necessary to include the subsection.

4. Provide the cite in proper *Bluebook* format to the 1968 United States Third Circuit Court of Appeals case applying the rule from Question 3 in which the court, in regards to affirmations and circumstances where they may be made in lieu of oath, held that where the party is a follower of a minority religion which is unpopular with many people in the community, it is better to permit the party to affirm and have questions on the subject of their religion asked outside of the jury's presence.

5. Under Federal Rule of Criminal Procedure 14, before ruling on a defendant's motion to sever, what may the court order an attorney for the government to deliver to the court for in camera inspection?

6. Under the Federal Rules of Criminal Procedure, in regards to closing arguments, does the government argue before the defense?

7. Cite the rule from Question 6 in proper *Bluebook* format. When citing the rule, cite to the overall rule number. It is not necessary to include the subsection.

8. Provide the cite in proper *Bluebook* format to the 1977 United States Fifth Circuit Court of Appeals case applying the rule from Question 7 in which the court, in regards to closing arguments generally and reading from the transcript, held that the defense counsel was not entitled to make additional summations to the jury after the jury requested that certain evidence be reread, and the court did not err in refusing defense counsel more summations since the court properly followed the format for final arguments set out in the rules.

9. Under Federal Rule of Appellate Procedure 4, in a civil case, if one of the parties is the United States, the notice of appeal may be filed by any party within how many days after entry of the judgment or order appealed from?

10. Under the Federal Rules of Appellate Procedure, before a judgment of conviction in a criminal case, must the district court state in writing, or orally on the record, the reasons for an order regarding the release or detention of a defendant in a criminal case?

11. Cite the rule from Question 10 in proper *Bluebook* format. When citing the rule, cite to the overall rule number. It is not necessary to include the subsection.

12. Provide the cite in proper *Bluebook* format to the 1981 United States Fifth Circuit Court of Appeals case interpreting the rule from Question 11 in which the court held, in regard to the standards for release pending appeals from conviction, that the rule did not encompass appeal from order revoking probation.

Exercise D

1. Under Federal Rule of Civil Procedure 14, can any party move to strike a third-party claim?

2. Under the Federal Rules of Civil Procedure, the master's compensation must be paid from what sources?

3. Cite the rule from Question 2 in proper *Bluebook* format. When citing the rule, cite to the overall rule number. It is not necessary to include the subsection.

4. Provide the cite in proper *Bluebook* format to the 1993 United States Sixth Circuit Court of Appeals case applying the rule from Question 3 in which the court, in regards to congested calendars and appointments of masters, held that a congestion of the court calendar due to an increasing docket and shortage of "judge power" did not meet the "exceptional condition" requirement to warrant a referral to special master.

5. Under Federal Rule of Criminal Procedure 24, in a capital case, how many peremptory challenges is each side entitled to have in regards to prospective jurors (not including alternate jurors)?

6. Under the Federal Rules of Criminal Procedure, must the court arrest judgment if the court does not have jurisdiction of the charged offense?

7. Cite the rule from Question 6 in proper *Bluebook* format. When citing the rule, cite to the overall rule number. It is not necessary to include the subsection.

8. Provide the cite in proper *Bluebook* format to the 1977 United States District Court for the Western District of Oklahoma case applying the rule from Question 7 in which the court, in regards to jurisdiction generally and grounds for relief, held that a motion in arrest of judgment must be based upon the failure of indictment to charge an offense or upon a finding that the court lacks jurisdiction of the offense.

9. Under Federal Rule of Appellate Procedure 8, must a party ordinarily move first in the district court for the approval of a supersedeas bond?

10. Under the Federal Rules of Appellate Procedure, for an intervention, does a person who files a motion for leave to intervene with the circuit clerk have to serve a copy on all parties?

11. Cite the rule from Question 10 in proper *Bluebook* format. When citing the rule, cite to the overall rule number. It is not necessary to include the subsection.

12. Provide the cite in proper *Bluebook* format to the 1983 United States Fifth Circuit Court of Appeals case interpreting the rule from Question 11 in which the court, in regards to proper parties, held that the Director of the Office of Workers' Compensation Programs is considered a proper party respondent before the Court of Appeals.

Exercise E

1. Under Federal Rule of Civil Procedure 21, is misjoinder of parties a ground for dismissing an action?

2. Under the Federal Rules of Civil Procedure, is the setting aside of default judgements allowed?

3. Cite the rule from Question 2 in proper *Bluebook* format. When citing the rule, cite to the overall rule number. It is not necessary to include the subsection.

4. Provide the cite in proper *Bluebook* format to the 1975 United States District Court for the Northern District of Georgia case applying the rule from Question 3 in which the court, in regards to excusable neglect and setting aside a default or a default judgment, held that when setting aside a default as opposed to vacating a default judgment, it is not always necessary that the neglect or oversight be excusable.

5. Under Federal Rule of Criminal Procedure 32, in regards to the presentence investigation, if the law allows restitution, what must the probation officer do after conducting an investigation?

6. Under the Federal Rules of Criminal Procedure, when may a person who commits criminal contempt be punished for that contempt?

7. Cite the rule from Question 6 in proper *Bluebook* format. When citing the rule, cite to the overall rule number. It is not necessary to include the subsection.

8. Provide the cite in proper *Bluebook* format to the 1998 United States Fifth Circuit Court of Appeals case applying the rule from Question 7 in which the court, in regards to a failure to appear or absences constituting contempt, held that a judgment debtor could not be punished summarily for criminal contempt based upon her absence from the deposition and hearing, since the contempt was not committed in the court's presence.

9. Under Federal Rule of Appellate Procedure 10, is the transcript of the proceedings the only item included in the record on appeal?

10. Under the Federal Rules of Appellate Procedure, does a single judge have the power to entertain a motion?

11. Cite the rule from Question 10 in proper *Bluebook* format. When citing the rule, cite to the overall rule number. It is not necessary to include the subsection.

12. Provide the cite in proper *Bluebook* format to the 1985 United States Tenth Circuit Court of Appeals case interpreting the rule from Question 11 in which the court, in regards to single judge actions and the authority of single judges in these actions, held that a single-judge order denying defendants' motion to dismiss appeal was simply a procedural order requiring appeal to be placed on the calendar and briefed, not a determination that would have a preclusive effect on the issue of the validity of the appeal.

Exercise F

1. Under Federal Rule of Civil Procedure 25, if a party becomes incompetent, what may a court, on motion, do?

2. Under the Federal Rules of Civil Procedure, when must the court disregard harmless errors that do not affect any party's substantial rights?

3. Cite the rule from Question 2 in proper *Bluebook* format. When citing the rule, cite to the overall rule number. It is not necessary to include the subsection.

4. Provide the cite in proper *Bluebook* format to the 1982 United States Eighth Circuit Court of Appeals case applying the rule from Question 3 in which the court, in regards to instructions generally, held that the harmless error rule applied to jury instructions as well as to other alleged errors.

5. Under Federal Rule of Criminal Procedure 49, must a party file with the court a copy of any paper they are required to serve?

6. Under the Federal Rules of Criminal Procedure, in regards to schedules, must preference be given to criminal proceedings as far as practicable so that there is a prompt disposition?

7. Cite the rule from Question 6 in proper *Bluebook* format. When citing the rule, cite to the overall rule number. It is not necessary to include the subsection.

8. Provide the cite in proper *Bluebook* format to the 1973 United States Second Circuit Court of Appeals case applying the rule from Question 7 in which the court, in regards to notice of readiness and calendars, held that the Government's filing of notice of readiness does not foreclose defendants being able to assert that the Government was not, in fact, ready.

9. Under Federal Rule of Appellate Procedure 11, if, before the record is forwarded, a party makes a motion for release in the court of appeals, must the district clerk send the court of appeals any parts of the record designated by any party?

10. Under the Federal Rules of Appellate Procedure, within how many days after the record is filed must the appellant complete service of a brief?

11. Cite the rule from Question 10 in proper *Bluebook* format. When citing the rule, cite to the overall rule number. It is not necessary to include the subsection.

12. Provide the cite in proper *Bluebook* format to the 1985 United States Second Circuit Court of Appeals case interpreting the rule from Question 11 in which the court, in regards to extension of time to file and good cause, held that motions to extend time to file briefs will be carefully scrutinized and will be denied unless "good cause" is shown, and "good cause" will not be deemed to exist unless movant offers something more than normal, or even reasonably anticipated but abnormal, vicissitudes inherent in the practice of law.

Assignment Ten
Chapter 13
ADMINISTRATIVE LAW

GOALS:

• Introduce you to locating proposed federal regulations.

• Familiarize you with finding federal regulations by subject and identifying Source notes and Authority notes.

• Give you an opportunity to update a regulation using *LSA: List of CFR Sections Affected.*

• Provide practice finding and citing Presidential proclamations.

CITATION:

♦ For purposes of Assignment Ten, assume you are writing a legal document and citing the law in citations and not textual sentences. Consequently, follow the typeface conventions in Bluepages B2.

♦ Use *Bluebook* Rule 14 to cite to administrative and executive materials and Rule 14.4 when citing administrative materials found in a commercial electronic database. Review tables T1, T6, T10, and T12 for guidance. In particular, see the information under "Executive Office of the President" in table T1.2 Federal Administrative Materials for information on citing Presidential proclamations.

♦ Use *Bluebook* Rule 10 to cite cases. Apply the abbreviation rules in 10.2.2 and use table T6. Tables T1 and T10 will also be useful. Unless specifically instructed to do so, do not include information as to prior or subsequent history weight of authority.

♦ Even if you are not instructed to give the complete cite in proper *Bluebook* format, use *Bluebook* abbreviations in your answers.

SOURCES USED:

OTHER SOURCES:

Print

Online

Federal Register
LSA: List of CFR Sections Affected
Code of Federal Regulations

Lexis Advance
Bloomberg Law
FDsys
HeinOnline

Online

WestlawNext [LSA not available]

EXAMPLE EXERCISE:

1. Find the *Federal Register* for December 9, 2014. Look at the proposed regulation on page 72998 and provide the cite in proper *Bluebook* format. Include the name of the regulation.

   > **Proposed Establishment of Class E Airspace; Tucumcari, N.M., 79 Fed. Reg. 72,998 (proposed Dec. 9, 2014) (to be codified at 14 C.F.R. pt. 71).**

2. The Consumer Product Safety Commission has issued consumer protection regulations concerning the safety standard for bicycle helmets. Locate the regulations in the *Code of Federal Regulations*. What is the purpose and basis for the standard?

   > **The purpose and basis is to reduce the likelihood of serious injury and death to bicyclists resulting from impacts to the head.**

3. For the regulation in Question 2, provide the cite in proper *Bluebook* format to the regulation section in the most recent edition of the *Code of Federal Regulations*. Do not include the name of the regulation.

   > **16 C.F.R. § 1203.2 (2014).**
   >
   > **Note: The year in the cite will change annually.**

4. Find the Source note for the regulation in Question 3. In proper *Bluebook* format, give the cite to the regulation as published in the *Federal Register*. Do not include the name of the regulation or the codification information.

   > **63 Fed. Reg. 11,729 (Mar. 10, 1998).**

5. Find the Authority note for the regulation in Question 3. Give the cite to the federal statutes where Congress gave the agency the power to promulgate the regulation. Omit the references to subpart B and subpart C.

   > **15 U.S.C. §§ 2056, 2058, and 6001-6006**

6. Provide the cite in proper *Bluebook* format to the 2013 Presidential proclamation on Constitution Day, Citizenship Day, and Constitution Week.

> **Print answer:**
> **Proclamation No. 9019, 3 C.F.R. 127-128 (2013).**
>
> **3 C.F.R. Index:**
> **Constitution Day and Citizenship Day, Constitution Week**
>
> *WestlawNext* **answer:**
> **Proclamation No. 9019, 78 Fed. Reg. 57,779 (Sept. 16, 2013).**

7. Use the *LSA: List of CFR Sections Affected* for March 2015. Determine if any change occurred in 17 C.F.R. § 449.1. What is the status of that section? **Note**: The LSA is not available on *WestlawNext*.

> **Amended**

8. Still using the *LSA*, on what page of volume 79 of the *Federal Register* published in 2014, would you find this change?

> **Page 38,456**

Exercise A

1. Find the *Federal Register* for April 1, 2013. Look at the proposed regulation on page 19431 and provide the cite in proper *Bluebook* format. Include the name of the regulation.

2. The National Science Foundation has issued regulations concerning Antarctica and the collection of Antarctic meteorites. Locate the regulations in the *Code of Federal Regulations*. What restrictions have been placed on the collection of meteorites in Antarctica?

3. For the regulation in Question 2, provide the cite in proper *Bluebook* format to the regulation section in the most recent edition of the *Code of Federal Regulations*. Do not include the name of the regulation.

4. Find the Source note for the regulation in Question 3. In proper *Bluebook* format, give the cite to the regulation as published in the *Federal Register*. Do not include the name of the regulation or the codification information.

5. Find the Authority note for the regulation in Question 3. Give the cite to the federal statutes where Congress gave the agency the power to promulgate the regulation.

6. Provide the cite in proper *Bluebook* format to the 2013 Presidential proclamation on Irish-American Heritage Month.

7. Use the *LSA: List of CFR Sections Affected* for January 2015. Determine if any change occurred in 38 C.F.R. § 3.151. What is the status of that section? **Note**: The LSA is not available on *WestlawNext*.

8. Still using the *LSA*, on what page of volume 79 of the *Federal Register* published in 2014, would you find this change?

Exercise B

1. Find the *Federal Register* for March 16, 2012. Look at the proposed regulation on page 15650 and provide the cite in proper *Bluebook* format. Include the name of the regulation.

2. The Federal Aviation Administration has issued regulations concerning agricultural aircraft operations. Locate the regulations in the *Code of Federal Regulations*. Under the operating rules relating to aircraft requirements, an aircraft cannot be operated unless the aircraft is equipped with what device?

3. For the regulation in Question 2, provide the cite in proper *Bluebook* format to the regulation section in the most recent edition of the *Code of Federal Regulations*. Do not include the name of the regulation.

4. Find the Source note for the regulation in Question 3. In proper *Bluebook* format, give the cite to the regulation as published in the June 24, 1965 *Federal Register*. Do not include the name of the regulation or the codification information.

5. Find the Authority note for the regulation in Question 3. Give the cite to the federal statutes where Congress gave the agency the power to promulgate the regulation.

6. Provide the cite in proper *Bluebook* format to the 2013 Presidential proclamation on Law Day, U.S.A.

7. Use the *LSA: List of CFR Sections Affected* for February 2015. Determine if any change occurred in 36 C.F.R. § 51.11. What is the status of that section? **Note**: The LSA is not available on *WestlawNext*.

8. Still using the *LSA*, on what page of volume 79 of the *Federal Register* published in 2014, would you find this change?

Exercise C

1. Find the *Federal Register* for October 7, 2014. Look at the proposed regulation on page 60383 and provide the cite in proper *Bluebook* format. Include the name of the regulation.

2. The Department of the Army has issued regulations concerning military court fees. Locate the regulations in the *Code of Federal Regulations*. In general, how is the use of the term "court" construed?

3. For the regulation in Question 2, provide the cite in proper *Bluebook* format to the regulation section in the most recent edition of the *Code of Federal Regulations*. Do not include the name of the regulation.

4. Find the Source note for the regulation in Question 3. In proper *Bluebook* format, give the cite to the regulation as published in the *Federal Register*. Do not include the name of the regulation or the codification information.

5. Find the Authority note for the regulation in Question 3. Give the cite to the federal statute where Congress gave the agency the power to promulgate the regulation.

6. Provide the cite in proper *Bluebook* format to the 2013 Presidential proclamation on Great Outdoors Month.

7. Use the *LSA: List of CFR Sections Affected* for March 2015. Determine if any change occurred in 39 C.F.R. § 601.113. What is the status of that section? **Note**: The LSA is not available on *WestlawNext*.

8. Still using the *LSA*, on what page of volume 79 of the *Federal Register* published in 2014, would you find this change?

Exercise D

1. Find the *Federal Register* for February 19, 2015. Look at the proposed regulation on page 8821 and provide the cite in proper *Bluebook* format. Include the name of the regulation.

2. The Office of the Secretary of the Interior has issued regulations concerning historic preservation and the preservation of American antiquities. Locate the regulations in the *Code of Federal Regulations*. Over what lands does the Secretary of Agriculture exercise jurisdiction over ruins?

3. For the regulation in Question 2, provide the cite in proper *Bluebook* format to the regulation section in the most recent edition of the *Code of Federal Regulations*. Do not include the name of the regulation.

4. Find the Source note for the regulation in Question 3. In proper *Bluebook* format, give the cite to the regulation as published in the *Federal Register*. Do not include the name of the regulation or the codification information.

5. Find the Authority note for the regulation in Question 3. Give the cite to the federal statute where Congress gave the agency the power to promulgate the regulation.

6. Provide the cite in proper *Bluebook* format to the 2013 Presidential proclamation on American Education Week.

7. Use the *LSA: List of CFR Sections Affected* for April 2015. Determine if any change occurred in 28 C.F.R. § 25.2. What is the status of that section? **Note**: The LSA is not available on *WestlawNext*.

8. Still using the *LSA*, on what page of volume 79 of the *Federal Register* published in 2014, would you find this change?

Exercise E

1. Find the *Federal Register* for March 4, 2015. Look at the proposed regulation on page 11614 and provide the cite in proper *Bluebook* format. Include the name of the regulation.

2. The Federal Highway Administration has issued regulations concerning electronic toll collection. Locate the regulations in the *Code of Federal Regulations*. What is the definition of electronic toll collection?

3. For the regulation in Question 2, provide the cite in proper *Bluebook* format to the regulation section in the most recent edition of the *Code of Federal Regulations*. Do not include the name of the regulation.

4. Find the Source note for the regulation in Question 3. In proper *Bluebook* format, give the cite to the regulation as published in the October 8, 2009 *Federal Register*. Do not include the name of the regulation or the codification information.

5. Find the Authority note for the regulation in Question 3. Give the cite to the federal statutes where Congress gave the agency the power to promulgate the regulation.

6. Provide the cite in proper *Bluebook* format to the 2013 Presidential proclamation on Wright Brothers Day.

7. Use the *LSA: List of CFR Sections Affected* for January 2015. Determine if any change occurred in 50 C.F.R. § 21.43. What is the status of that section? **Note**: The LSA is not available on *WestlawNext*.

8. Still using the *LSA*, on what page of volume 79 of the *Federal Register* published in 2014, would you find this change?

Assignment Ten, Chapter 13, Exercise F

Exercise F

1. Find the *Federal Register* for March 5, 2015. Look at the proposed regulation on page 11968 and provide the cite in proper *Bluebook* format. Include the name of the regulation.

2. The Forest Service has issued regulations concerning national forests and cave resources management. Locate the regulations in the *Code of Federal Regulations*. In regards to purpose and scope, to what do the rules apply?

3. For the regulation in Question 2, provide the cite in proper *Bluebook* format to the regulation in the most recent edition of the *Code of Federal Regulations*. Do not include the name of the regulation.

4. Find the Source note for the regulation in Question 3. In proper *Bluebook* format, give the cite to the regulation as published in the *Federal Register*. Do not include the name of the regulation or the codification information.

5. Find the Authority note for the regulation in Question 3. Give the cite to the federal statutes where Congress gave the agency the power to promulgate the regulation.

6. Provide the cite in proper *Bluebook* format to the 2013 Presidential proclamation on Bill of Rights Day.

7. Use the *LSA: List of CFR Sections Affected* for February 2015. Determine if any change occurred in 22 C.F.R. § 13.1. What is the status of that section? **Note**: The LSA is not available on *WestlawNext*.

8. Still using the *LSA*, on what page of volume 79 of the *Federal Register* published in 2014, would you find this change?

Assignment Eleven
Chapter 15
CITATORS

GOALS:
• Practice updating law using *KeyCite* on *WestlawNext* and *Shepard's* on *Lexis Advance*.
• Familiarize you with verifying cases and expanding your research.
• Introduce you to the Table of Authorities feature in online citators.

CITATION:

♦ For purposes of Assignment Eleven, assume you are writing a legal document and citing the law in citations and not textual sentences. Consequently, follow the typeface conventions in Bluepages B2.

♦ Use *Bluebook* Rule 10 to cite cases. Apply the abbreviation rules in 10.2.2 and use table T6. Tables T1 and T10 will also be useful. Unless specifically instructed to do so, do not include information as to prior or subsequent history weight of authority.

♦ Use *Bluebook* Rule 16 and table T13 to cite law review articles.

♦Even if you are not instructed to give the complete cite in proper *Bluebook* format, use *Bluebook* abbreviations in your answers.

SOURCES:

<u>Online</u>

This assignment was written to use these online citators:

KeyCite on *WestlawNext*
Shepard's on *Lexis Advance*

EXAMPLE EXERCISE:

Your research has brought you to a United States Court of Appeals decision *United States v. Barbosa*, 906 F.2d 1366 (9th Cir. 1990). KeyCite the case and answer the following questions.

1. Defendant-Appellant Barbosa attempted to appeal to the Supreme Court of the United States. What was the result of his petition?
    Certiorari denied

2. What is the cite to the Supreme Court of the United States decision in the official reports from Question 1?
    498 U.S. 961

3. Does 906 F.2d 1399 have any negative direct history?
    No

4. Look at the negative citing references for 906 F.2d 1366. Give the cite in proper *Bluebook* format to the 1997 Third Circuit decision that disagreed with *Barbosa*.
    ***United States v. Arnold*, 106 F.3d 37 (3d Cir. 1997).**

5. In proper *Bluebook* format, give the cite to the 1993 Ninth Circuit decision whose depth of treatment **examined** *Barbosa*. Do not include a pinpoint cite.
    ***United States v. Worthy*, 988 F.2d 126 (9th Cir. 1993).**

6. In proper *Bluebook* format, give the cite to the 2009 Ninth Circuit decision that cites *Barbosa* for the point of law in Headnote 2 (*Controlled Substances* key number 79). In your cite, include a pinpoint cite to the first page of the discussion.
    ***United States v. Ahearn*, 310 F. App'x 199, 201 (9th Cir. 2009).**

KeyCite the Supreme Court of the United States decision *Bowen v. Galbreath*, 485 U.S. 74 (1998) and answer the following questions.

7. Look at the negative citing references for 485 U.S. 74. Give the cite in proper *Bluebook* format to the 1994 Federal Circuit decision that declined to extend *Galbreath*.
    ***In re Fee Agreement of Wick*, 40 F.3d 7 (Fed. Cir. 1994).**

8. Under Citing References, find and cite in proper *Bluebook* format, the 1995 article in the Administrative Law Review that cites *Galbreath*.

   Alison M. MacDonald & Victor Williams, *In Whose Interests? Evaluating Attorneys' Fee Awards and Contingent-Fee Agreements in Social Security Disability Benefits Cases*, 47 Admin. L. Rev. 115 (1995).

9. Has the law review article from Question 8 been cited in any law-related documents or journals?

   Yes

10. Look at the Table of Authorities for 485 U.S. 74. How many cases are relied upon as authority in *Galbreath*?

    9

    In your research you found a United States Court of Appeals decision *United States v. Davis*, 905 F.2d 245 (9th Cir. 1990). Shepardize the case and answer the following questions.

11. Defendant-Appellant Davis attempted to appeal to the Supreme Court of the United States. What was the result of his petition?

    Certiorari denied

12. What is the cite to the Supreme Court of the United States decision in the official reports from Question 11?

    498 U.S. 1047

13. Does 905 F.2d 245 have any negative subsequent appellate history?

    No

14. Look at the citing decisions for 905 F.2d 245. Give the cite in proper *Bluebook* format to the 1992 United States District Court decision that criticized *Davis*.

    United States v. Juda, 797 F. Supp. 774 (N.D. Cal. 1992).

15. In proper *Bluebook* format, give the cite to the 2008 Ninth Circuit decision whose depth of discussion **analyzed** *Davis*. Do not include a pinpoint cite.

    United States v. Lei Shi, 525 F.3d 709 (9th Cir. 2008).

16. In proper *Bluebook* format, give the cite to the 2011 Second Circuit decision that cites *Davis* for the point of law in LexisNexis Headnote 7 (found on the Lexis online version of the case). In your cite, include a pinpoint cite to the page where first cited.
United States v. Al Kassar, 660 F.3d 108, 118 (2d Cir. 2011).

Shepardize the Supreme Court of the United States decision Forest Grove School District v. T.A., 557 U.S. 230 (2008) and answer the following questions.

17. Look at the citing decisions for 557 U.S. 230. Give the cite in proper *Bluebook* format to the 2012 Seventh Circuit decision that distinguished *Forest Grove School District v. T.A.*
Jamie S. v. Milwaukee Pub. Schs., 668 F.3d 481 (7th Cir. 2012).

18. Under Other Citing Sources, find and cite in proper *Bluebook* format, the 2014 article in the Capital University Law Review that cites *Forest Grove School District v. T.A.*
Elizabeth Adamo Usman, *Reality Over Ideology: A Practical View of Special Needs Voucher Programs*, 42 Cap. U. L. Rev. 53 (2014).

19. Has the law review article from Question 8 been cited in any law-related documents or journals?
Yes

20. Look at the Table of Authorities for 557 U.S. 230. How many cases are cited in *Forest Grove School District v. T.A.*?
16

Exercise A

Your research has brought you to a United States Court of Appeals decision *United States v. Polk*, 905 F.2d 54 (4th Cir. 1990). KeyCite the case and answer the following questions.

1. Defendant-appellant Polk attempted to appeal to the Supreme Court of the United States. What was the result of his petition?

2. What is the cite to the Supreme Court of the United States decision in the official reports from Question 1?

3. Does 905 F.2d 54 have any negative direct history?

4. Look at the negative citing references for 905 F.2d 54. Give the cite in proper *Bluebook* format to the 2014 Fourth Circuit decision where *Polk* was not followed as dicta.

5. In proper *Bluebook* format, give the cite to the 2013 Fourth Circuit decision whose depth of treatment **discussed** *Polk*. Do not include a pinpoint cite.

6. In proper *Bluebook* format, give the cite to the 1997 Fourth Circuit decision that cites *Polk* for the point of law in Headnote 1 (*Sentencing and Punishment* key number 664(2)). In your cite, include a pinpoint cite to the first page of the discussion unless the first page of discussion is also the first page of the case.

KeyCite the Supreme Court of the United States decision *Carroll v. United States*, 354 U.S. 394 (1957) and answer the following questions.

7. Look at the negative citing references for 354 U.S. 394. Give the cite in proper *Bluebook* format to the 1997 Tenth Circuit decision that indicated Carroll was superseded by statute.

8. Under Citing References, find and cite in proper *Bluebook* format, the 1997 article in the Notre Dame Law Review that cites *Carroll.*

9. Has the law review article from Question 8 been cited in any law-related documents or journals?

10. Look at the Table of Authorities for 354 U.S. 394. How many cases are relied upon as authority in *Carroll?*

In your research you found a United States Court of Appeals decision *United States v. Campuzano*, 905 F.2d 677 (2d Cir. 1990). Shepardize the case and answer the following questions.

11. Defendants-Appellants Campuzano and Rios attempted to appeal to the Supreme Court of the United States. What was the result of their petition?

12. What is the cite to the Supreme Court of the United States decision in the official reports from Question 11?

13. Does 905 F.2d 677 have any negative subsequent appellate history?

14. Look at the citing decisions for 905 F.2d 677. Give the cite in proper *Bluebook* format to the 1992 United States District Court decision that stated that *Campuzano* had been overruled in part.

15. In proper *Bluebook* format, give the cite to the 1991 Second Circuit decision whose depth of discussion **analyzed** *Campuzano*. Do not include a pinpoint cite.

16. In proper *Bluebook* format, give the cite to the 2005 Second Circuit decision that cites *Campuzano* for the point of law in LexisNexis Headnote 6 (found on the Lexis online version of the case). In your cite, include a pinpoint cite to the page where first cited.

Shepardize the Supreme Court of the United States decision *Marino v. Ortiz*, 484 U.S. 301 (1988) and answer the following questions.

17. Look at the citing decisions for 484 U.S. 301. Give the cite in proper *Bluebook* format to the 2002 Supreme Court of the United States decision that distinguished *Marino v. Ortiz*.

18. Under Other Citing Sources, find and cite in proper *Bluebook* format, the 2012 article in the Florida State University Law Review that cites *Marino v. Ortiz*.

19. Has the law review article from Question 8 been cited in any law-related documents or journals?

20. Look at the Table of Authorities for 484 U.S. 301. How many cases are cited in *Marino v. Ortiz*?

Exercise B

Your research has brought you to a United States Court of Appeals decision *Gantner v. Commissioner*, 905 F.2d 241 (8th Cir. 1990). KeyCite the case and answer the following questions.

1. Gantner attempted to appeal to the Supreme Court of the United States. What was the result of his petition?

2. What is the cite to the Supreme Court of the United States decision in the official reports from Question 1?

3. Does 905 F.2d 241 have any negative direct history?

4. Look at the negative citing references for 905 F.2d 241. Give the cite in proper *Bluebook* format to the 1990 Tax Court decision that indicated *Gantner* was superseded by statute.

5. In proper *Bluebook* format, give the cite to the 1993 Tax Court decision whose depth of treatment **discussed** *Gantner*. Do not include a pinpoint cite.

6. In proper *Bluebook* format, give the cite to the 2003 Eighth Circuit decision that cites *Gantner* for the point of law in Headnote 4 (*Internal Revenue* key number 3395). In your cite, include a pinpoint cite to the first page of the discussion.

KeyCite the Supreme Court of the United States decision *Vanderbilt v. Vanderbilt*, 354 U.S. 416 (1957) and answer the following questions.

7. Look at the negative citing references for 354 U.S. 416. Give the cite in proper *Bluebook* format to the 1981 Court of Appeals of Louisiana decision that distinguished *Vanderbilt*.

8. Under Citing References, find and cite in proper *Bluebook* format, the 1990 article in the American Journal of Legal History that cites *Vanderbilt*.

9. Has the law review article from Question 8 been cited in any law-related documents or journals?

10. Look at the Table of Authorities for 354 U.S. 416. How many cases are relied upon as authority in *Vanderbilt*?

In your research you found a United States Court of Appeals decision *Saturn Distribution Corp. v. Williams*, 905 F.2d 719 (4th Cir. 1990). Shepardize the case and answer the following questions.

11. Petitioner Williams attempted to appeal to the Supreme Court of the United States. What was the result of his petition?

12. What is the cite to the Supreme Court of the United States decision in the official reports from Question 11?

13. Does 905 F.2d 719 have any negative subsequent appellate history?

14. Look at the citing decisions for 905 F.2d 719. Give the cite in proper *Bluebook* format to the 2003 Supreme Court of Florida decision that distinguished *Saturn Distribution Corp.*

15. In proper *Bluebook* format, give the cite to the 1992 Fourth Circuit decision whose depth of discussion **analyzed** *Saturn Distribution Corp.* Do not include a pinpoint cite.

16. In proper *Bluebook* format, give the cite to the 1997 Fourth Circuit decision that cites *Saturn Distribution Corp.* for the point of law in LexisNexis Headnote 4 (found on the Lexis online version of the case). In your cite, include a pinpoint cite to the page where first cited.

Shepardize the Supreme Court of the United States decision *Taylor v. Illinois*, 484 U.S. 400 (1988) and answer the following questions.

17. Look at the citing decisions for 484 U.S. 400. Give the cite in proper *Bluebook* format to the 1995 First Circuit decision that distinguished *Taylor v. Illinois*.

18. Under Other Citing Sources, find and cite in proper *Bluebook* format, the 2014 article in the Alabama Law Review that cites *Taylor v. Illinois*.

19. Has the law review article from Question 8 been cited in any law-related documents or journals?

20. Look at the Table of Authorities for 484 U.S. 400. How many cases are cited in *Taylor v. Illinois*?

Exercise C

Your research has brought you to a United States Court of Appeals decision *United States v. Davis*, 905 F.2d 245 (9th Cir. 1990). KeyCite the case and answer the following questions.

1. Defendant Davis attempted to appeal to the Supreme Court of the United States. What was the result of his petition?

2. What is the cite to the Supreme Court of the United States decision in the official reports from Question 1?

3. Does 905 F.2d 245 have any negative direct history?

4. Look at the negative citing references for 905 F.2d 245. Give the cite in proper *Bluebook* format to the 1999 First Circuit decision that disagreed with *Davis*.

5. In proper *Bluebook* format, give the cite to the 2006 Ninth Circuit decision whose depth of treatment **examined** *Davis*. Do not include a pinpoint cite.

6. In proper *Bluebook* format, give the cite to the 1993 Third Circuit decision that declines to follow *Davis* for the point of law in Headnote 6 (*Constitutional Law* key number 4560). In your cite, include a pinpoint cite to the first page of the discussion.

   KeyCite the Supreme Court of the United States decision *Wilson v. Girard*, 354 U.S. 524 (1957) and answer the following questions.

7. Look at the negative citing references for 345 U.S. 524. Give the cite in proper *Bluebook* format to the 2009 Central District of California decision that distinguished from *Girard*.

8. Under Citing References, find and cite in proper *Bluebook* format, the 2004 article in the Arizona State Law Journal that cites *Girard*.

9. Has the law review article from Question 8 been cited in any law-related documents or journals?

10. Look at the Table of Authorities for 354 U.S. 524. How many cases are relied upon as authority in *Girard*?

In your research you found a United States Court of Appeals decision *United States v. Hall*, 905 F.2d 959 (6th Cir. 1990). Shepardize the case and answer the following questions.

11. Defendant-Appellant Hall attempted to appeal to the Supreme Court of the United States. What was the result of his petition?

12. What is the cite to the Supreme Court of the United States decision in the official reports from Question 11?

13. Does 905 F.2d 959 have any negative subsequent appellate history?

14. Look at the citing decisions for 905 F.2d 959. Give the cite in proper *Bluebook* format to the 2008 Court of Appeals of Maryland decision that criticized *Hall*.

15. In proper *Bluebook* format, give the cite to the 2001 Court of Special Appeals of Maryland decision whose depth of discussion **discussed** *Hall*. Do not include a pinpoint cite.

16. In proper *Bluebook* format, give the cite to the 2000 Eighth Circuit decision that cites *Hall* for the point of law in LexisNexis Headnote 1 (found on the Lexis online version of the case). In your cite, include a pinpoint cite to the page where first cited.

Shepardize the Supreme Court of the United States decision *United States v. Fausto*, 484 U.S. 439 (1988) and answer the following questions.

17. Look at the citing decisions for 484 U.S. 439. Give the cite in proper *Bluebook* format to the 2012 Federal Circuit decision that indicates *Fausto* has been superseded by statute.

18. Under Other Citing Sources, find and cite in proper *Bluebook* format, the 2002 article in the Arizona State Law Journal that cites *Fausto*.

19. Has the law review article from Question 8 been cited in any law-related documents or journals?

20. Look at the Table of Authorities for 484 U.S. 439. How many cases are cited in *Fausto*?

Exercise D

Your research has brought you to a United States Court of Appeals decision *Carbray v. Champion*, 905 F.2d 314 (10th Cir. 1990). KeyCite the case and answer the following questions.

1. Petitioner-Appellant Carbray attempted to appeal to the Supreme Court of the United States. What was the result of his petition?

2. What is the cite to the Supreme Court of the United States decision in the official reports from Question 1?

3. Does 905 F.2d 314 have any negative direct history?

4. Look at the negative citing references for 905 F.2d 314. Give the cite in proper *Bluebook* format to the 2009 Tenth Circuit decision that distinguished from *Carbray*.

5. In proper *Bluebook* format, give the cite to the 1990 Oklahoma Court of Criminal Appeals decision whose depth of treatment **discussed** *Carbray*. Do not include a pinpoint cite.

6. In proper *Bluebook* format, give the cite to the 2004 Tenth Circuit decision that cites *Carbray* for the point of law in Headnote 2 (*Criminal Law* key number 749). In your cite, include a pinpoint cite to the first page of the discussion.

KeyCite the Supreme Court of the United States decision *Calbeck v. Travelers Insurance Co.*, 370 U.S. 114 (1962) and answer the following questions.

7. Look at the negative citing references for 370 U.S. 114. Give the cite in proper *Bluebook* format to the 1991 Fourth Circuit decision that indicates *Calbeck* was superseded by statute.

8. Under Citing References, find and cite in proper *Bluebook* format, the 2003 article in the Journal of Maritime Law and Commerce that cites *Calbeck*.

9. Has the law review article from Question 8 been cited in any law-related documents or journals?

10. Look at the Table of Authorities for 370 U.S. 114. How many cases are relied upon as authority in *Calbeck*?

In your research you found a United States Court of Appeals decision *United States v. Paiz*, 905 F.2d 1014 (7th Cir. 1990). Shepardize the case and answer the following questions.

11. Defendants-Appellants Paiz and Rector attempted to appeal to the Supreme Court of the United States. What was the result of his petition?

12. What is the cite to the Supreme Court of the United States decision in the official reports from Question 11?

13. Does 905 F.2d 1014 have any negative subsequent appellate history?

14. Look at the citing decisions for 905 F.2d 1014. Give the cite in proper *Bluebook* format to the 1996 First Circuit decision that criticized *Paiz*.

15. In proper *Bluebook* format, give the cite to the 1997 District of Nebraska decision whose depth of discussion **analyzed** *Paiz*. Do not include a pinpoint cite.

16. In proper *Bluebook* format, give the cite to the 2000 Seventh Circuit decision that cites *Paiz* for the point of law in LexisNexis Headnote 2 (found on the Lexis online version of the case). In your cite, include a pinpoint cite to the page where first cited.

Shepardize the Supreme Court of the United States decision *United States v. Owens*, 484 U.S. 554 (1988) and answer the following questions.

17. Look at the citing decisions for 484 U.S. 554. Give the cite in proper *Bluebook* format to the 2009 Seventh Circuit decision that distinguished *Owens*.

18. Under Other Citing Sources, find and cite in proper *Bluebook* format, the 2001 article in the Columbia Law Review that cites *Owens*.

19. Has the law review article from Question 8 been cited in any law-related documents or journals?

20. Look at the Table of Authorities for 484 U.S. 554. How many cases are cited in *Owens*?

Exercise E

Your research has brought you to a United States Court of Appeals decision *Drabkin v. Alexander Grant & Co.*, 905 F.2d 453 (D.C. Cir. 1990). KeyCite the case and answer the following questions.

1. Appellee Drabkin attempted to appeal to the Supreme Court of the United States. What was the result of his petition?

2. What is the cite to the Supreme Court of the United States decision in the official reports from Question 1?

3. Does 905 F.2d 453 have any negative direct history?

4. Look at the negative citing references for 905 F.2d 453. Give the cite in proper *Bluebook* format to the 2002 Appellate Court of Illinois decision that distinguished from *Drabkin*.

5. In proper *Bluebook* format, give the cite to the 2012 Southern District of New York decision whose depth of treatment **examined** *Drabkin*. Do not include a pinpoint cite.

6. In proper *Bluebook* format, give the cite to the 2004 Northern District of Illinois decision that cites *Drabkin* for the point of law in Headnote 1 (*Accountants* key number 8). In your cite, include a pinpoint cite to the first page of the discussion.

   KeyCite the Supreme Court of the United States decision *Taylor v. Louisiana*, 370 U.S. 154 (1962) and answer the following questions.

7. Look at the negative citing references for 370 U.S. 154. Give the cite in proper *Bluebook* format to the 1964 Supreme Court of Mississippi decision that distinguished from *Taylor*.

175

8. Under Citing References, find and cite in proper *Bluebook* format, the 2009 article in the American University Law Review that cites *Taylor*.

9. Has the law review article from Question 8 been cited in any law-related documents or journals?

10. Look at the Table of Authorities for 370 U.S. 154. How many cases are relied upon as authority in *Taylor*?

In your research you found a United States Court of Appeals decision *United States v. Dobynes*, 905 F.2d 1192 (8th Cir. 1990). Shepardize the case and answer the following questions.

11. Appellant Dobynes attempted to appeal to the Supreme Court of the United States. What was the result of his petition?

12. What is the cite to the Supreme Court of the United States decision in the official reports from Question 11?

13. Does 905 F.2d 1192 have any negative subsequent appellate history?

14. Look at the citing decisions for 905 F.2d 1192. Give the cite in proper *Bluebook* format to the 1999 Eighth Circuit decision that distinguished *Dobynes*.

15. In proper *Bluebook* format, give the cite to the 2008 Eighth Circuit decision whose depth of discussion **mentioned** *Dobynes*. Do not include a pinpoint cite.

16. In proper *Bluebook* format, give the cite to the 2000 Eighth Circuit decision that cites *Dobynes* for the point of law in LexisNexis Headnote 1 (found on the Lexis online version of the case). In your cite, include a pinpoint cite to the page where first cited.

Shepardize the Supreme Court of the United States decision *United States v. Robinson*, 485 U.S. 25 (1988) and answer the following questions.

17. Look at the citing decisions for 485 U.S. 25. Give the cite in proper *Bluebook* format to the 1988 Sixth Circuit decision that distinguished *Robinson*.

18. Under Other Citing Sources, find and cite in proper *Bluebook* format, the 1990 article in the Indiana Law Journal that cites *Robinson*.

19. Has the law review article from Question 8 been cited in any law-related documents or journals?

20. Look at the Table of Authorities for 485 U.S. 25. How many cases are cited in *Robinson*?

Exercise F

Your research has brought you to a United States Court of Appeals decision *Benjamin v. Coughlin*, 905 F.2d 571 (2d Cir. 1990). KeyCite the case and answer the following questions.

1. Defendant-Appellee Coughlin attempted to appeal to the Supreme Court of the United States. What was the result of the petition?

2. What is the cite to the Supreme Court of the United States decision in the official reports from Question 1?

3. Does 905 F.2d 571 have any negative direct history?

4. Look at the negative citing references for 905 F.2d 571. Give the cite in proper *Bluebook* format to the 1990 Tenth Circuit decision that disapproved of *Benjamin*.

5. In proper *Bluebook* format, give the cite to the 1993 Second Circuit decision whose depth of treatment **discussed** *Benjamin*. Do not include a pinpoint cite.

6. In proper *Bluebook* format, give the cite to the 1991 Second Circuit decision that cites *Benjamin* for the point of law in Headnote 3 (*Judgment* key number 828). In your cite, include a pinpoint cite to the first page of the discussion.

KeyCite the Supreme Court of the United States decision *Wood v. Georgia*, 370 U.S. 375 (1962) and answer the following questions.

7. Look at the negative citing references for 370 U.S. 375. Give the cite in proper *Bluebook* format to the 2005 Ninth Circuit decision that distinguished *Wood*.

8. Under Citing References, find and cite in proper *Bluebook* format, the 1997 article in the Arkansas Law Review that cites *Wood*.

9. Has the law review article from Question 8 been cited in any law-related documents or journals?

10. Look at the Table of Authorities for 370 U.S. 375. How many cases are relied upon as authority in *Wood*?

In your research you found a United States Court of Appeals decision *United States v. Gardner*, 905 F.2d 1432 (10th Cir. 1990). Shepardize the case and answer the following questions.

11. Defendant-Appellant Gardner attempted to appeal to the Supreme Court of the United States. What was the result of his petition?

12. What is the cite to the Supreme Court of the United States decision in the official reports from Question 11?

13. Does 905 F.2d 1432 have any negative subsequent appellate history?

14. Look at the citing decisions for 905 F.2d 1432. Give the cite in proper *Bluebook* format to the 1994 Tenth Circuit decision that distinguished *Gardner*.

15. In proper *Bluebook* format, give the cite to the 1990 Tenth Circuit decision whose depth of discussion **analyzed** *Gardner*. Do not include a pinpoint cite.

16. In proper *Bluebook* format, give the cite to the 1998 Tenth Circuit decision that cites *Gardner* for the point of law in LexisNexis Headnote 2 (found on the Lexis online version of the case). In your cite, include a pinpoint cite to the page where first cited.

Shepardize the Supreme Court of the United States decision *Mathews v. United States*, 485 U.S. 58 (1998) and answer the following questions.

17. Look at the citing decisions for 485 U.S. 58. Give the cite in proper *Bluebook* format to the 2011 Tenth Circuit decision that critisized *Mathews*.

18. Under Other Citing Sources, find and cite in proper *Bluebook* format, the 2004 article in the Connecticut Law Review that cites *Mathews*.

19. Has the law review article from Question 8 been cited in any law-related documents or journals?

20. Look at the Table of Authorities for 557 U.S. 230. How many cases are cited in *Mathews*?

Assignment Twelve
Chapter 16
LEGAL ENCYCLOPEDIAS

GOALS:

• Introduce you to finding commentary in legal encyclopedias.

• Provide practice in locating primary authority in legal encyclopedias.

CITATION:

♦ **For purposes of Assignment Twelve, assume you are citing the legal encyclopedias and cases in citations in a legal document, and not in textual sentences. Consequently, follow the typeface conventions in Bluepages B2.**

♦ **Use *Bluebook* Rule 15.8(a) for citing legal encyclopedias and Rule 10 to cite cases. Apply the abbreviation rules in 10.2.2 and use table T6. Tables T1 and T10 will also be useful. Unless specifically instructed to do so, do not include information as to prior or subsequent history weight of authority.**

♦ **Refer to Rule 15.9 if you are researching on *WestlawNext* or *Lexis Advance*.**

♦**Even if you are not instructed to give the complete cite in proper *Bluebook* format, use *Bluebook* abbreviations in your answers.**

SOURCES:

<u>Print</u>

Questions 2-9:
Corpus Juris Secundum (C.J.S.)

Questions 10-17:
American Jurisprudence 2d (Am. Jur. 2d)

<u>Online</u>

Questions 2-9:
Corpus Juris Secundum (C.J.S.) on *WestlawNext*

Questions 10-17:
American Jurisprudence 2d (Am. Jur. 2d) on *WestlawNext* or *Lexis Advance*

EXAMPLE EXERCISE:

1. Determine if your state has a legal encyclopedia. If so, what is the name of the publication?
   Answers will vary depending on your state.

For Questions 2-9, use *Corpus Juris Secundum* if available.

2. Is the game of football, or the operation of the stadium for the game, a nuisance per se if conducted in a reasonable manner?
   No

3. Give the cite in proper *Bluebook* format to the encyclopedia entry that answers Question 2.
   66 C.J.S. *Nuisances* § 58 (2009).

4. In proper *Bluebook* format, give the cite to the 1946 Kentucky case that supports the answer in Question 2.
   ***Bd. of Educ. of Louisville v. Klein*, 197 S.W.2d 427 (Ky. 1946).**

5. Give the West Key Number Digest topic and key numbers that you can use to find additional cases with the subject matter of the encyclopedia entry in Question 3.
   ***Nuisance* key numbers 3(9) and 61**

6. Examine the topic outline for the topic *Entertainment and Amusement; Sports*. Under which section would you find information on the general considerations for personal injuries relating to the sport of golf?
   Section 97

7. Go to the section from Question 6. Does a golfer about to take his shot have a duty to warn another player who is aware of the imminence of the golfer's shot?
   No

8. Give the cite in proper *Bluebook* format to the encyclopedia entry that answers Question 7.
   30A C.J.S. *Entertainment and Amusement; Sports* § 97 (2007).

9. In proper *Bluebook* format, give the cite to the 1984 Arizona Court of Appeals case that supports the answer in Question 7.
Cook v. Johnston, 688 P.2d 215 (Ariz. Ct. App. 1984).

For Questions 10-17, use *American Jurisprudence 2d* if available.

10. Are states permitted to prohibit the sale of intoxicating liquors during the hours of the day when a school election is being held?
Yes

11. Give the cite in proper *Bluebook* format to the encyclopedia entry that answers Question 10.
45 Am. Jur. 2d *Intoxicating Liquors* § 227 (2007).

12. In proper *Bluebook* format, give the cite to the 1941 Arizona Supreme Court case that supports the answer in Question 10.
State v. Blazina, 120 P.2d 395 (Ariz. 1941).

13. Give the West Key Number Digest topic and key number that you can use to find additional cases with the subject matter of the encyclopedia entry in Question 11.
Intoxicating Liquors key number 120

14. Examine the topic outline for the topic *Schools*. Under which section would you find information on requiring teachers to take loyalty oaths as part of the qualifications for hire?
Section 167

15. Go to the section from Question 14. May a school constitutionally require a teacher to take an oath that he or she will support the federal and state constitutions?
Yes

16. Give the cite in proper *Bluebook* format to the encyclopedia entry that answers Question 15.
67B Am. Jur. 2d *Schools* § 167 (2010).

17. In proper *Bluebook* format, give the cite to the 1995 Superior Court of New Jersey, Appellate Division case that supports the answer in Question 15.
Gough v. State, 667 A.2d 1057 (N.J. Super. Ct. App. Div. 1995).

Exercise A

1. Determine if your state has a legal encyclopedia. If so, what is the name of the publication?

   For Questions 2-9, use _Corpus Juris Secundum_ if available.

2. When trying to determine libel, is dictation of libelous matter to a stenographer considered a publication in some jurisdictions?

3. Give the cite in proper _Bluebook_ format to the encyclopedia entry that answers Question 2.

4. In proper _Bluebook_ format, give the cite to the 1901 Maryland case that supports the answer in Question 2.

5. Give the West Key Number Digest topic and key numbers that you can use to find additional cases with the subject matter of the encyclopedia entry in Question 3.

6. Examine the topic outline for the topic _Game; Conservation and Preservation of Wildlife_. Under which section would you find information about whether a game warden is considered a law enforcement officer?

7. Go to the section from Question 6. Are game wardens and game rangers usually empowered to arrest violators of the game laws?

8. Give the cite in proper _Bluebook_ format to the encyclopedia entry that answers Question 7.

9. In proper _Bluebook_ format, give the cite to the 1988 Court of Criminal Appeals of Oklahoma case that supports the answer in Question 7.

For Questions 10-17, use *American Jurisprudence 2d* if available.

10. Trailer parks may not be a nuisance per se, but can such an establishment become a nuisance by the manner it was operated?

11. Give the cite in proper *Bluebook* format to the encyclopedia entry that answers Question 10.

12. In proper *Bluebook* format, give the cite to the 1989 Georgia Court of Appeals case that supports the answer in Question 10.

13. Give the West Key Number Digest topic and key numbers that you can use to find additional cases with the subject matter of the encyclopedia entry in Question 11.

14. Examine the topic outline for the topic *Newspapers, Periodicals, and Press Associations*. Under which section would you find information on liabilities of publishers for mistakes in news reports or items?

15. Go to the section from Question 14. If a news story does not contain libel, will any action for damages lie against a newspaper for merely inaccurate reporting?

16. Give the cite in proper *Bluebook* format to the encyclopedia entry that answers Question 15.

17. In proper *Bluebook* format, give the cite to the 1986 Ohio Supreme Court case that supports the answer in Question 15.

Exercise B

1. Determine if your state has a legal encyclopedia. If so, what is the name of the publication?

    For Questions 2-9, use *Corpus Juris Secundum* if available.

2. Does the state have the burden of proving all of the material elements of the crime in order to convict a person of the crime of bribery?

3. Give the cite in proper *Bluebook* format to the encyclopedia entry that answers Question 2.

4. In proper *Bluebook* format, give the cite to the 1923 Ohio case that supports the answer in Question 2.

5. Give the West Key Number Digest topic and key numbers that you can use to find additional cases with the subject matter of the encyclopedia entry in Question 3.

6. Examine the topic outline for the topic *Weapons*. Under which section would you find information on regulating whether certain persons could be prohibited from carrying, possessing, or owning weapons under the Constitution?

7. Go to the section from Question 6. Can the Second Amendment's right to keep and bear arms be limited by statutes that prohibit the carrying or possession of weapons by particular classes of persons including mentally ill persons?

8. Give the cite in proper *Bluebook* format to the encyclopedia entry that answers Question 7.

9. In proper *Bluebook* format, give the cite to the 2008 United States Supreme Court case that supports the answer in Question 7.

For Questions 10-17, use *American Jurisprudence 2d* if available.

10. May a launderer or dry cleaner have a contract with a customer to limit his liability to that customer?

11. Give the cite in proper *Bluebook* format to the encyclopedia entry that answers Question 10.

12. In proper *Bluebook* format, give the cite to the 1921 Georgia Court of Appeals case that supports the answer in Question 10.

13. Give the West Key Number Digest topics and key numbers that you can use to find additional cases with the subject matter of the encyclopedia entry in Question 11.

14. Examine the topic outline for the topic *Logs and Timber*. Under which section would you find information on liability in the logging industry for floating loose logs as a means of transportation?

15. Go to the section from Question 14. Does a person have the right to use navigable streams to float loose logs?

16. Give the cite in proper *Bluebook* format to the encyclopedia entry that answers Question 15.

17. In proper *Bluebook* format, give the cite to the 1910 Arkansas Supreme Court case that supports the answer in Question 15.

Exercise C

1. Determine if your state has a legal encyclopedia. If so, what is the name of the publication?

   For Questions 2-9, use *Corpus Juris Secundum* if available.

2. When distinguishing a bounty from a reward, is the term reward usually applied to a sum paid to a person or persons for a specific act?

3. Give the cite in proper *Bluebook* format to the encyclopedia entry that answers Question 2.

4. In proper *Bluebook* format, give the cite to the 1894 Fifth Circuit case that supports the answer in Question 2.

5. Give the West Key Number Digest topic and key numbers that you can use to find additional cases with the subject matter of the encyclopedia entry in Question 3.

6. Examine the topic outline for the topic *Cemeteries*. Under which section would you find information on civil liability for trespassing or other offenses in a cemetery?

7. Go to the section from Question 6. Can a person who desecrates or wrongfully invades burial grounds or the burial lot of another be sued for damages?

8. Give the cite in proper *Bluebook* format to the encyclopedia entry that answers Question 7.

9. In proper *Bluebook* format, give the cite to the 1936 Alabama Supreme Court case that supports the answer in Question 7.

For Questions 10-17, use *American Jurisprudence 2d* if available.

10. In cases of emotional distress, does the "zone of danger" liability test limit the damages for mental anguish to plaintiffs who sustain a physical injury due to defendant's negligent conduct or who are placed in immediate risk of physical harm by plaintiff's conduct?

11. Give the cite in proper *Bluebook* format to the encyclopedia entry that answers Question 10.

12. In proper *Bluebook* format, give the cite to the 2008 Alabama Supreme Court case that supports the answer in Question 10.

13. Give the West Key Number Digest topic and key numbers that you can use to find additional cases with the subject matter of the encyclopedia entry in Question 11.

14. Examine the topic outline for the topic *Passports*. Under which section would you find information generally on the denial or revocation of a passport?

15. Go to the section from Question 14. The Secretary of State may deny or revoke a person's passport if his conduct abroad causes or is likely to cause serious damage to the national security of the United States. Does an applicant's conduct abroad have to be illegal to be grounds for denial of a passport?

16. Give the cite in proper *Bluebook* format to the encyclopedia entry that answers Question 15.

17. In proper *Bluebook* format, give the cite to the 1981 Supreme Court case that supports the answer in Question 15.

Exercise D

1. Determine if your state has a legal encyclopedia. If so, what is the name of the publication?

   For Questions 2-9, use *Corpus Juris Secundum* if available.

2. When an accused, who is out on bail, willfully fails to appear or violates any other conditions of a release order, can the court properly impose the sanction of contempt as a penalty?

3. Give the cite in proper *Bluebook* format to the encyclopedia entry that answers Question 2.

4. In proper *Bluebook* format, give the cite to the 1982 Arizona Supreme Court case that supports the answer in Question 2.

5. Give the West Key Number Digest topic and key numbers that you can use to find additional cases with the subject matter of the encyclopedia entry in Question 3.

6. Examine the topic outline for the topic *Husband and Wife*. Under which section would you find information on what constitutes separate property?

7. Go to the section from Question 6. Does property acquired by a person before marriage remain that person's separate property?

8. Give the cite in proper *Bluebook* format to the encyclopedia entry that answers Question 7.

9. In proper *Bluebook* format, give the cite to the 2001 North Carolina Court of Appeals case that supports the answer in Question 7.

For Questions 10-17, use *American Jurisprudence 2d* if available.

10. Can a veterinarian's license be revoke or suspended for violating FDA regulations of illegal animal drugs?

11. Give the cite in proper *Bluebook* format to the encyclopedia entry that answers Question 10.

12. In proper *Bluebook* format, give the cite to the 1991 Iowa Supreme Court case that supports the answer in Question 10.

13. Give the West Key Number Digest topics and key numbers that you can use to find additional cases with the subject matter of the encyclopedia entry in Question 11.

14. Examine the topic outline for the topic *Inspection Laws*. Under which section would you find information on certificates on inspection and inspection tags under the administration of inspection laws in general?

15. Go to the section from Question 14. Do inspection laws often provide for the placing of tags on inspected products to show the result of inspections?

16. Give the cite in proper *Bluebook* format to the encyclopedia entry that answers Question 15.

17. In proper *Bluebook* format, give the cite to the 1957 Texas Court of Criminal Appeals case that supports the answer in Question 15.

Exercise E

1. Determine if your state has a legal encyclopedia. If so, what is the name of the publication?

   For Questions 2-9, use *Corpus Juris Secundum* if available.

2. Does the presumption of death apply when a person's unexplainable absence can only be explained by assuming death?

3. Give the cite in proper *Bluebook* format to the encyclopedia entry that answers Question 2.

4. In proper *Bluebook* format, give the cite to the 1945 Minnesota Supreme Court case that supports the answer in Question 2.

5. Give the West Key Number Digest topic and key number that you can use to find additional cases with the subject matter of the encyclopedia entry in Question 3.

6. Examine the topic outline for the topic *Embezzlement*. Under which section would you find general information on the origin and nature of the offense of embezzlement?

7. Go to the section from Question 6. Is it true that embezzlement may be an ongoing offense where a person was in continuous receipt of money embezzling different amounts at different times?

8. Give the cite in proper *Bluebook* format to the encyclopedia entry that answers Question 7.

9. In proper *Bluebook* format, give the cite to the 1944 Missouri Supreme Court case that supports the answer in Question 7.

For Questions 10-17, use *American Jurisprudence 2d* if available.

10. If title to public land has passed under federal law, is the property subject to state law relating to liens?

11. Give the cite in proper *Bluebook* format to the encyclopedia entry that answers Question 10.

12. In proper *Bluebook* format, give the cite to the 1887 Wisconsin Supreme Court case that supports the answer in Question 10.

13. Give the West Key Number Digest topic and key number that you can use to find additional cases with the subject matter of the encyclopedia entry in Question 11.

14. Examine the topic outline for the topic *Witnesses*. Under which section would you find information on the duty of testifying even though it may degrade or disgrace the witness?

15. Go to the section from Question 14. Can the witness refuse to testify if the answers will degrade or disgrace him when the answers are collateral to the issue being tried?

16. Give the cite in proper *Bluebook* format to the encyclopedia entry that answers Question 15.

17. In proper *Bluebook* format, give the cite to the 1975 Georgia Supreme Court case that supports the answer in Question 15.

Exercise F

1. Determine if your state has a legal encyclopedia. If so, what is the name of the publication?

   For Questions 2-9, use *Corpus Juris Secundum* if available.

2. Is it a duty of a sheriff generally to arrest any persons committing or attempting to commit a public offense?

3. Give the cite in proper *Bluebook* format to the encyclopedia entry that answers Question 2.

4. In proper *Bluebook* format, give the cite to the 1993 Fifth Circuit case that supports the answer in Question 2.

5. Give the West Key Number Digest topic and key numbers that you can use to find additional cases with the subject matter of the encyclopedia entry in Question 3.

6. Examine the topic outline for the topic *Electricity*. Under which section would you find information about electric companies and tree trimming near lines?

7. Go to the section from Question 6. Does an electric company have the authority to remove trees under its lines where it is reasonably necessary to accomplish the purpose of the easement?

8. Give the cite in proper *Bluebook* format to the encyclopedia entry that answers Question 7.

9. In proper *Bluebook* format, give the cite to the 2013 Georgia Court of Appeals case that supports the answer in Question 7.

For Questions 10-17, use *American Jurisprudence 2d* if available.

10. In a criminal trial, is it generally appropriate to give a missing-witness instruction to a jury when a an undercover police office is not called to testify?

11. Give the cite in proper *Bluebook* format to the encyclopedia entry that answers Question 10.

12. In proper *Bluebook* format, give the cite to the 1979 Eighth Circuit case that supports the answer in Question 10.

13. Give the West Key Number Digest topics and key numbers that you can use to find additional cases with the subject matter of the encyclopedia entry in Question 11.

14. Examine the topic outline for the topic *Zoning and Planning*. Under which section would you find information on zoning regulations for beaches?

15. Go to the section from Question 14. If land that is contiguous to a beach is considered unique, can it subsequently be subject to more restrictive zoning regulations than other property?

16. Give the cite in proper *Bluebook* format to the encyclopedia entry that answers Question 15.

17. In proper *Bluebook* format, give the cite to the 1973 New Jersey Supreme Court case that supports the answer in Question 15.

Assignment Thirteen
Chapter 17
AMERICAN LAW REPORTS (A.L.R.)

GOALS:
• Provide practice in locating *American Law Reports*.
• Introduce you to the features of the *American Law Reports*.

CITATION:

♦For purposes of Assignment Thirteen, assume you are citing the *American Law Reports* annotations and cases in citations in a legal document, and not in textual sentences. Consequently, follow the typeface conventions in Bluepages B2.

♦Use *Bluebook* Rule 16.7.6 for citing *American Law Report (A.L.R.)* annotations and Rule 10 to cite cases. Apply the abbreviation rules in 10.2.2 and use table T6. Tables T1 and T10 will also be useful. Unless specifically instructed to do so, do not include information as to prior or subsequent history weight of authority.

♦Even if you are not instructed to give the complete cite in proper *Bluebook* format, use *Bluebook* abbreviations in your answers.

SOURCES:

<u>Print</u>

American Law Reports

<u>Online</u>

WestlawNext*
Lexis Advance

*We highly recommend using *WestlawNext* over *Lexis Advance* when researching *American Law Reports* for these exercises.

EXAMPLE EXERCISE:

1. An ionscan is a device used to detect very small quantities of illegal drugs. Find and retrieve an American Law Reports annotation that discusses the admissibility of ionscan evidence. Provide the cite in proper *Bluebook* format to the 2004 annotation in print.
    Marjorie A. Shields, Annotation, *Admissibility of Ion Scan Evidence*, 124 A.L.R.5th 691 (2004).

2. Provide the cite in proper *Bluebook* format of the 2002 United States District Court case named at the beginning of the annotation that is representative of the subject of the annotation.
    United States v. Lake, 233 F. Supp. 2d 465 (E.D.N.Y. 2002).

3. Look at the Research References for the annotation. Under West Digest Key Numbers, what are the key numbers under topic *Controlled Substances* that you could use to locate court decisions on this subject?
    Key numbers 117, 146, and 184

4. Look at the Index. What section of the annotation discusses Rule of Evidence 702?
    Section 6

5. Look at the Jurisdictional Table of Cited Statutes and Cases (called Table of Cases, Laws, and Rules on *WestlawNext*). What section of the annotation cites 21 U.S.C.A. § 881(b)?
    Section 4

6. What section of the annotation cites to a 1994 First Circuit decision?
    Section 6

7. Give the cite in proper *Bluebook* format to the 1994 First Circuit decision cited in the section from Question 6.
    United States v. Romero, 32 F.3d 641 (1st Cir. 1994).

8. Give the cite in proper *Bluebook* format to the 2003 Alaska decision cited in the annotation.
    McGee v. State, 70 P.3d 429 (Alaska Ct. App. 2003).

9. Read the Scope of the annotation as given under the Introduction. Would this be a good annotation to read if you were researching cases where courts considered the admissibility of ion scan evidence?
    Yes

10. You need to know how the courts apply the Federal Employees Health Benefits Act (FEHBA). Find an American Law Reports annotation that discusses this issue. Provide the cite in proper *Bluebook* format to the 2006 annotation in print.

> **James Lockhart, Annotation, *Validity, Construction, and Application of Federal Employees Health Benefits Act (FEHBA), 5 U.S.C.A. §§ 8901 to 8914*, 8 A.L.R. Fed. 2d 1 (2006).**

11. Provide the cite in proper *Bluebook* format of the 2002 Ninth Circuit case named at the beginning of the annotation that is representative of the subject of the annotation.

> **Roach v. Mail Handlers Benefit Plan, 298 F.3d 847 (9th Cir. 2002).**

12. Look at the Research References for the annotation. Under West's Key Number Digest, what are the key numbers under topic *Insurance* that you could use to locate court decisions on this subject?

> **Key numbers 1109 and 1117(3)**

13. Look at the Index. What section of the annotation discusses debarment proceedings?

> **Section 81**

14. Look at the Table of Cases (called Jurisdictional Table of Statutes and Cases on *Lexis Advance*). What section of the annotation cites to the Supreme Court of the United States decision *Pegram v. Herdrich*?

> **Section 23**

15. What section of the annotation cites to a 2000 Sixth Circuit decision?

> **Section 53**

16. Give the cite in proper *Bluebook* format to the 2000 Sixth Circuit decision cited in the section from Question 15.

> **Stonitsch v. United States, 238 F.3d 424 (6th Cir. 2000).**

Exercise A

1. Find and retrieve an American Law Reports annotation that discusses liability for misappropriation of trade secrets and conversion of genetic material. Provide the cite in proper *Bluebook* format to the 2004 annotation in print.

2. Provide the cite in proper *Bluebook* format of the 2003 United States District Court case named at the beginning of the annotation that is representative of the subject of the annotation.

3. Look at the Research References for the annotation. Under West Digest Key Numbers, what are the key numbers under topic *Torts* that you could use to locate court decisions on this subject?

4. Look at the Index. What section of the annotation discusses Informed Consent?

5. Look at the Jurisdictional Table of Cited Statutes and Cases (called Table of Cases, Laws, and Rules on *WestlawNext*). What section of the annotation cites Fla. Stat. Ann. § 760.40?

6. What section of the annotation cites to a 1994 Eighth Circuit decision out of Iowa?

7. Give the cite in proper *Bluebook* format to the 1994 Eighth Circuit decision cited in the section from Question 6.

8. Give the cite in proper *Bluebook* format to the 2004 North Carolina Court of Appeals decision cited in the annotation.

9. Read the Scope of the annotation as given under the Introduction. Would this be a good annotation to read if you were researching cases in which courts have determined whether liability for conversion or misappropriation of genetic material was established or supportable?

10. You need to know how the courts are addressing the form and sufficiency of copyright notices. Find an American Law Reports annotation that discusses this issue. Provide the cite in proper *Bluebook* format to the 2007 annotation in print.

11. Provide the cite in proper *Bluebook* format of the 2004 Second Circuit case named at the beginning of the annotation that is representative of the subject of the annotation.

12. Look at the Research References for the annotation. Under West's Key Number Digest, what are the key numbers under topic *Copyrights and Intellectual Property* that you could use to locate court decisions on this subject?

13. Look at the Index. What sections of the annotation discuss videotapes?

14. Look at the Table of Cases. What section of the annotation cites to the 1891 Supreme Court of the United States decision *Higgins v. Keuffel*?

15. What section of the annotation cites to a 1985 Fifth Circuit decision?

16. Give the cite in proper *Bluebook* format to the 1985 Fifth Circuit decision cited in the section from Question 15.

Exercise B

1. Find and retrieve an American Law Reports annotation that discusses the actions by or against individuals or groups protesting or picketing at funerals. Provide the cite in proper *Bluebook* format to the 2008 annotation in print.

2. Provide the cite in proper *Bluebook* format of the 2008 United States District Court case named at the beginning of the annotation that is representative of the subject of the annotation.

3. Look at the Research References for the annotation. Under West's Key Number Digest, what is the key number under topic *Disorderly Conduct* that you could use to locate court decisions on this subject?

4. Look at the Index. What sections of the annotation discuss floating buffer zones?

5. Look at the Table of Cases, Laws, and Rules. What section of the annotation cites 42 U.S.C.A. § 1988(b)?

6. What section of the annotation cites to a 1988 United States Supreme Court decision?

7. Give the cite in proper *Bluebook* format to the 1988 United States Supreme Court decision cited in the section from Question 6.

8. Give the cite in proper *Bluebook* format to the 2008 Kansas decision cited in the annotation.

9. Read the Scope of the annotation as given under Preliminary Matters. Would this be a good annotation to read if you were researching cases about requests for restraining orders against funeral picketers?

10. You need to know how the courts construct and apply the Resolution Trust Corporation Whistleblower Act. Find an American Law Reports annotation that discusses this issue. Provide the cite in proper *Bluebook* format to the 2008 annotation in print.

11. Provide the cite in proper *Bluebook* format of the 2005 District of Columbia Circuit case named at the beginning of the annotation that is representative of the subject of the annotation.

12. Look at the Research References for the annotation. Under West's Key Number Digest, what is the key number under topic *Constitutional Law* that you could use to locate court decisions on this subject?

13. Look at the Index. What sections of the annotation discuss gag orders?

14. Look at the Table of Cases. What section of the annotation cites to the 1993 Supreme Court of the United States decision *Hazen Paper Co. v. Biggins*?

15. What sections of the annotation cite to a 1995 District of Columbia Circuit decision?

16. Give the cite in proper *Bluebook* format to the 1995 District of Columbia Circuit decision cited in the section from Question 15.

Exercise C

1. Find and retrieve an American Law Reports annotation that discusses the action for tortious interference with bequest as precluded by will contest remedy. Provide the cite in proper *Bluebook* format to the 1994 annotation in print.

2. Provide the cite in proper *Bluebook* format of the 1992 Supreme Court of Iowa case named at the beginning of the annotation that is representative of the subject of the annotation.

3. Look at the Research References for the annotation. Under West Digest Key Numbers, what are the key numbers under topic *Wills* that you could use to locate court decisions on this subject?

4. Look at the Index. What sections of the annotation discuss Mental state of testator?

5. Look at the Jurisdictional Table of Cited Statutes and Cases (called Table of Cases, Laws, and Rules on *WestlawNext*). What sections of the annotation cite Fla. Stat. § 733.103(2)

6. What section of the annotation cites to a 1990 Missouri Court of Appeals decision?

7. Give the cite in proper *Bluebook* format to the 1990 Missouri Court of Appeals decision cited in the section from Question 6.

8. Give the cite in proper *Bluebook* format to the 1981 Florida Supreme Court decision cited in the annotation.

9. Read the Scope of the annotation as given under the Introduction. Would this be a good annotation to read if you were researching cases where the issue was whether, as a prerequisite to a tortious interference action, a claimant was obligated to bring and maintain a will contest proceeding?

10. You need to know how the courts construct and apply the Water Supply Act. Find an American Law Reports annotation that discusses this issue. Provide the cite in proper *Bluebook* format to the 2010 annotation in print.

11. Provide the cite in proper *Bluebook* format of the 2008 District of Columbia Circuit case named at the beginning of the annotation that is representative of the subject of the annotation.

12. Look at the Research References for the annotation. Under West's Key Number Digest, what is the key number under topic *Electricity* that you could use to locate court decisions on this subject?

13. Look at the Index. What section of the annotation discusses diversion from hydropower to local water supply use?

14. Look at the Table of Cases. What section of the annotation cites to the Third Circuit decision *Borough of Morrisville v. Delaware River Basin Commission*?

15. What section of the annotation cites to a 1981 Tenth Circuit decision?

16. Give the cite in proper *Bluebook* format to the 1981 Tenth Circuit decision cited in the section from Question 15.

Exercise D

1. Find and retrieve an American Law Reports annotation that discusses the validity, construction, and application of statutes prohibiting boating for pleasure while intoxicated or under the influence. Provide the cite in proper *Bluebook* format to the 2009 annotation in print.

2. Provide the cite in proper *Bluebook* format of the 2007 Supreme Court of Vermont case named at the beginning of the annotation that is representative of the subject of the annotation.

3. Look at the Research References for the annotation. Under West's Key Number Digest, what are the key numbers under topic *Searches and Seizures* that you could use to locate court decisions on this subject?

4. Look at the Index. What sections of the annotation discuss the absence of reasonable suspicion?

5. Look at the Table of Case, Laws, and Rules. What section of the annotation cites 14 U.S.C.A. § 89?

6. What section of the annotation cites to a 2000 Fourth Circuit decision?

7. Give the cite in proper *Bluebook* format to the 2000 Fourth Circuit decision cited in the section from Question 6.

8. Give the cite in proper *Bluebook* format to the 1988 Arkansas Court of Appeals decision cited in the annotation.

9. Read the Scope of the annotation as given under Preliminary Matters. Would this be a good annotation to read if you were researching cases about determining issues related to the collateral effects of a conviction for boating while intoxicated (BWI) or boating under the influence (BUI)?

10. You need to know how the courts apply copyright law to cookbooks, recipes, cooking shows, and the like. Find an American Law Reports annotation that discusses this issue. Provide the cite in proper *Bluebook* format to the 2012 annotation in print.

11. Provide the cite in proper *Bluebook* format of the 2007 United States District Court case named at the beginning of the annotation that is representative of the subject of the annotation.

12. Look at the Research References for the annotation. Under West's Key Number Digest, what are the key numbers under topic *Copyrights and Intellectual Property* that you could use to locate court decisions on this subject?

13. Look at the Index. What section of the annotation discusses icing recipes?

14. Look at the Table of Cases. What section of the annotation cites to the 1991 Supreme Court of the United States decision *Feist Publications, Inc. v. Rural Telephone Service Co.*?

15. What section of the annotation cites to a 1998 Sixth Circuit decision?

16. Give the cite in proper *Bluebook* format to the 1998 Sixth Circuit decision cited in the section from Question 15.

Exercise E

1. Find and retrieve an American Law Reports annotation that discusses the liability of building owners, lessees, or managers for injury or death resulting from the use of automatic passenger elevators. Provide the cite in proper *Bluebook* format to the 2002 annotation in print.

2. Provide the cite in proper *Bluebook* format of the 2000 Court of Appeals of Texas case named at the beginning of the annotation that is representative of the subject of the annotation.

3. Look at the Research References for the annotation. Under West Digest Key Numbers, what is the key number under topic *Evidence* that you could use to locate court decisions on this subject?

4. Look at the Index. What section of the annotation discusses Circumstantial Evidence?

5. Look at the Jurisdictional Table of Cited Statutes and Cases (called Table of Cases, Laws and Rules on *WestlawNext*). What sections of the annotation cite 28 U.S.C.A. § 1346(b)?

6. What sections of the annotation cite to a 1989 District of Columbia Circuit decision?

7. Give the cite in proper *Bluebook* format to the 1989 District of Columbia Circuit decision cited in the sections from Question 6.

8. Give the cite in proper *Bluebook* format to the 1981 Maine decision cited in the annotation.

9. Read the Scope of the annotation as given under the Introduction. Would this be a good annotation to read if you were researching cases in which the elevator was designed for operation by a trained attendant as opposed to push-button operation by any passenger?

10. You need to know how the courts determine civil liability under 18 U.S.C.A. § 2511(1)(a) for unauthorized interception or viewing of satellite television broadcasts. Find an American Law Reports annotation that discusses this issue. Provide the cite in proper *Bluebook* format to the 2011 annotation in print.

11. Provide the cite in proper *Bluebook* format of the 2008 Ninth Circuit case named at the beginning of the annotation that is representative of the subject of the annotation.

12. Look at the Research References for the annotation. Under West's Key Number Digest, what are the key numbers under topic *Telecommunications* that you could use to locate court decisions on this subject?

13. Look at the Index. What sections of the annotation discuss damages?

14. Look at the Table of Cases. What section of the annotation cites to the 2001 Fifth Circuit decision *Prostar v. Massachi*?

15. What section of the annotation cites to a 1995 Ninth Circuit decision?

16. Give the cite in proper *Bluebook* format to the 1995 Ninth Circuit decision cited in the section from Question 15.

Exercise F

1. Find and retrieve an American Law Reports annotation that discusses the effect, as between landlord and tenant, of a lease clause restricting the keeping of pets. Provide the cite in proper *Bluebook* format to the 2003 annotation in print.

2. Provide the cite in proper *Bluebook* format of the 2001 New York Supreme Court, Appellant Division case named at the beginning of the annotation that is representative of the subject of the annotation.

3. Look at the Research References for the annotation. Under West Digest Key Numbers, what are the key numbers under topic *Judgment* that you could use to locate court decisions on this subject?

4. Look at the Index. What section of the annotation discusses emotional, physical, or psychological dependence on pet?

5. Look at the Jurisdictional Table of Cited Statutes and Cases (called Table of Cases, Laws, and Rules on *WestlawNext*). What sections of the annotation cite 29 U.S.C.A. § 794?

6. What section of the annotation cites to a 2000 Northern District of California decision?

7. Give the cite in proper *Bluebook* format to the 2000 Northern District of California decision cited in the section from Question 6. **Note:** *WestlawNext* lists this case with 9th Circuit cases.

8. Give the cite in proper *Bluebook* format to the 1996 Colorado Court of Appeals decision cited in the annotation.

9. Read the Scope of the annotation as given under Preliminary Matters. Would this be a good annotation to read if you were researching cases in which the courts have considered, as between the landlord and tenant, the validity and enforceability of lease provisions that restrict having pets on the leased property?

10. You need to know how the courts constructed and applied statute of limitations applicable to prosecution under the federal murder-for-hire statute. Find an American Law Reports annotation that discusses this issue. Provide the cite in proper *Bluebook* format to the 2014 annotation in print.

11. Provide the cite in proper *Bluebook* format of the 2011 Eighth Circuit case named at the beginning of the annotation that is representative of the subject of the annotation.

12. Look at the Research References for the annotation. Under West's Key Number Digest, what are the key numbers under topic *Homicide* that you could use to locate court decisions on this subject?

13. Look at the Index. What section of the annotation discusses the tolling of statute of limitations?

14. Look at the Table of Cases. What sections of the annotation cite to the 1997 First Circuit decision *United States v. Owens*?

15. What sections of the annotation cite to a 1993 Fifth Circuit decision?

16. Give the cite in proper *Bluebook* format to the 1993 Fifth Circuit decision cited in the section from Question 15.

Assignment Fourteen
Chapter 18
LEGAL PERIODICALS

GOALS:
· Introduce you to finding commentary in legal encyclopedias.
· Provide practice in locating primary authority in legal encyclopedias.

CITATION:

♦For purposes of Assignment Fourteen, assume you are citing the legal periodicals and cases in citations in a legal document, and not in textual sentences. Consequently, follow the typeface conventions in Bluepages B2.

♦ Use *Bluebook* Rule 16 and table T13 for citing legal periodical articles and Rule 10 to cite cases. For case names, apply the abbreviation rules in 10.2.2 and use table T6. Tables T1 and T10 will also be useful. Unless specifically instructed to do so, do not include information as to prior or subsequent history weight of authority for cases.

♦Even if you are not instructed to give the complete cite in proper *Bluebook* format, use *Bluebook* abbreviations in your answers.

♦Although *Bluebook* Rule 16.8 gives direction on citing to electronic media and online sources, cite to the law review article in print for this assignment.

SOURCES: ## OTHER SOURCES:

Print   ### Online

Questions 1-3:   *HeinOnline*
Index to Legal Periodicals   *Bloomberg Law*
Current Law Index   *Index to Legal Periodicals Full Text*
                                         Google Scholar

Online

Questions 1-3
LegalTrac

Questions 4-10:
WestlawNext
Lexis Advance

EXAMPLE EXERCISE:

For Questions 1-3, use one of the periodical indexes: *Index to Legal Periodicals, Current Law Index,* or *LegalTrac.* Pull the article to cite it.

1. Locate the 2008 Florida Law Review article by Dana Remus Irwin and provide the cite in proper *Bluebook* format.

   Dana Remus Irwin, *Paradise Lost in the Patent Law? Changing Visions of Technology in the Subject Matter Inquiry,* **60 Fla. L. Rev. 775 (2008).**

2. Locate the 2007 Baylor Law Review article that analyzes *Anderson Producing Inc. v. Koch Oil Company,* 929 S.W.2d 416 (Tex. 1996). Provide the cite in proper *Bluebook* format. **Note**: This article is student written.

   Linda Jegermanis, Comment, *Danger at the Crossroads: Ethical Considerations for the Lawyer Seeking to Testify on Behalf of a Contingency Client After* **Anderson Producing Inc. v. Koch Oil Co., 59 Baylor L. Rev. 857 (2007).**

3. Locate the 2008 Fordham Law Review article about the glass ceiling and women attorneys. Provide the cite in proper *Bluebook* format.

   Judith S. Kaye & Anne C. Reddy, *The Progress of Women Lawyers at Big Firms: Steadied or Simply Studied?* **76 Fordham L. Rev. 1941 (2008).**

For Questions 4-6, use full-text search on *WestlawNext* or *Lexis Advance.* For your content on *WestlawNext,* you can limit your searches to Law Reviews & Journals in Secondary Sources. On *Lexis Advance,* you can filter by category. Select Secondary Materials.

4. Locate the 2009 Notre Dame Law Review article by Neil Duxbury and provide the cite in proper *Bluebook* format.

   Neil Duxbury, *Golden Rule Reasoning, Moral Judgment, and the Law,* **84 Notre Dame L. Rev. 1529 (2009).**

5. Locate the 2011 University of Colorado Law Review article that analyzes *Mesa County Board of County Commissioners v. State*, 203 P.3d 519 (Colo. 2009). Provide the cite in proper *Bluebook* format. **Note**: This article is student written.

> **Anna-Liisa Mullis, Comment, *Dismantling the Trojan Horse:* Mesa County Board of County Commissioners v. State, 82 U. Colo. L. Rev. 259 (2011).**

6. Locate the 2010 Cornell Law Review article about the fair use doctrine in the digital media environment. Provide the cite in proper *Bluebook* format.

> **Gideon Parchomovsky & Philip J. Weiser, *Beyond Fair Use*, 96 Cornell L. Rev. 91 (2010).**

Exercise A

For Questions 1-3, use one of the periodical indexes: *Index to Legal Periodicals, Current Law Index,* or *LegalTrac.* Pull the article to cite it.

1. Locate the 2008 North Carolina Law Review article by Paul Rose and provide the cite in proper *Bluebook* format.

2. Locate the 2009 University of Toledo Law Review article that analyzes *Robinson v. Bates*, 857 N.E.2d 1195 (Ohio 2005). Provide the cite in proper *Bluebook* format. **Note**: This article is student written.

3. Locate the 2008-2009 Journal of Law and Religion article about Muslim woman. Provide the cite in proper *Bluebook* format. (Some sources may indicate that this article was published in 2008 only.)

For Questions 4-6, use full-text search on *WestlawNext* or *Lexis Advance.* For your content on *WestlawNext*, you can limit your searches to Law Reviews & Journals in Secondary Sources. On *Lexis Advance*, you can filter by category. Select Secondary Materials.

4. Locate the 2011 Hastings Law Journal article by Ronald D. Rotunda and provide the cite in proper *Bluebook* format.

5. Locate the 2012 Saint Louis University Law Journal article that analyzes *Baldwin v. Fischer-Smith*, 315 S.W.3d 389 (Mo. Ct. App. 2010). Provide the cite in proper *Bluebook* format. **Note**: This article is student written.

6. Locate the 2011 Rutgers Law Review article about the duty of Congress to declare war. Provide the cite in proper *Bluebook* format.

Exercise B

For Questions 1-3, use one of the periodical indexes: *Index to Legal Periodicals*, *Current Law Index*, or *LegalTrac*. Pull the article to cite it.

1. Locate the 2006 Alabama Law Review article by Steven J. Cleveland and provide the cite in proper *Bluebook* format.

2. Locate the 2006 South Texas Law Review article that analyzes *Frye v. Kansas City Missouri Police Department*, 375 F.3d 785 (8th Cir. 2004). Provide the cite in proper *Bluebook* format. **Note**: This article is student written.

3. Locate the 2006 Penn State Law Review article about early childhood education and Project Head Start. Provide the cite in proper *Bluebook* format.

For Questions 4-6, use full-text search on *WestlawNext* or *Lexis Advance*. For your content on *WestlawNext*, you can limit your searches to Law Reviews & Journals in Secondary Sources. On *Lexis Advance*, you can filter by category. Select Secondary Materials.

4. Locate the 2010 Rutgers Law Journal article by Amnon Lehavi and provide the cite in proper *Bluebook* format.

5. Locate the 2012 Southern Illinois University Law Journal article that analyzes *United States v. Reyes-Hernandez*, 624 F.3d 405 (7th Cir. 2010). Provide the cite in proper *Bluebook* format. **Note**: This article is student written.

6. Locate the 2010 Harvard Environmental Law Review article about the disposal of spent nuclear fuel. Provide the cite in proper *Bluebook* format.

Exercise C

For Questions 1-3, use one of the periodical indexes: *Index to Legal Periodicals, Current Law Index,* **or** *LegalTrac.* **Pull the article to cite it.**

1. Locate the 2005 Saint Louis University Law Journal article by Harold S. Lewis, Jr. and provide the cite in proper *Bluebook* format.

2. Locate the 2004 Oklahoma City University Law Review article that analyzes *Bazzetta v. McGinnis*, 286 F.3d 311 (6th Cir. 2002). Provide the cite in proper *Bluebook* format. **Note**: This article is student written.

3. Locate the 2006 Villanova Sports & Entertainment Law Journal article about liability for sports accidents, particularly those involving horsemanship. Provide the cite in proper *Bluebook* format.

For Questions 4-6, use full-text search on *WestlawNext* **or** *Lexis Advance.* **For your content on** *WestlawNext,* **you can limit your searches to Law Reviews & Journals in Secondary Sources. On** *Lexis Advance,* **you can filter by category. Select Secondary Materials.**

4. Locate the 2011 Washington Law Review article by Robert C. Farrell and provide the cite in proper *Bluebook* format.

5. Locate the 2014 Texas Tech Law Review article that explores the problems with Texas' civil asset forfeiture system. Provide the cite in proper *Bluebook* format. **Note**: This article is student written.

6. Locate the 2007 Louisiana Law Review article about behavioral science and consumer standard form contracts. Provide the cite in proper *Bluebook* format.

Exercise D

For Questions 1-3, use one of the periodical indexes: *Index to Legal Periodicals, Current Law Index,* or *LegalTrac*. Pull the article to cite it.

1. Locate the 2005 Buffalo Law Review article by Philip C. Kissam and provide the cite in proper *Bluebook* format.

2. Locate the 2005 Baylor Law Review article that analyzes *Healthcare Centers, Inc. v. Rigby*, 97 S.W.3d 610 (Tex. App. 2002). Provide the cite in proper *Bluebook* format. **Note**: This article is student written.

3. Locate the 2005 Indiana Law Review article about firing or shooting ranges. Provide the cite in proper *Bluebook* format.

For Questions 4-6, use full-text search on *WestlawNext* or *Lexis Advance*. For your content on *WestlawNext*, you can limit your searches to Law Reviews & Journals in Secondary Sources. On *Lexis Advance*, you can filter by category. Select Secondary Materials.

4. Locate the 2013 Texas Law Review article by Daniel A. Crane and provide the cite in proper *Bluebook* format.

5. Locate the 2010 University of Dayton Law Review article that analyzes *KSR International Co. v. Teleflex Inc.*, 550 U.S. 398 (2007). Provide the cite in proper *Bluebook* format. **Note**: This article is student written.

6. Locate the 2012 Seton Hall Law Review article about attorneys intentionally inflicting emotional distress. Provide the cite in proper *Bluebook* format.

Exercise E

For Questions 1-3, use one of the periodical indexes: *Index to Legal Periodicals, Current Law Index,* or *LegalTrac.* Pull the article to cite it.

1. Locate the 2004 Florida State University Law Review article by Paul M. Secunda and provide the cite in proper *Bluebook* format.

2. Locate the 2004 University of Baltimore Law Review article that analyzes *Project Life, Inc. v. Glendening,* 139 F. Supp. 2d 703 (D. Md.2001). Provide the cite in proper *Bluebook* format. **Note**: This article is student written.

3. Locate the 2003 Arizona State Law Journal article about law students' undergraduate grades (scholastic marks) and law school admissions tests as predicting law school academic performance. Provide the cite in proper *Bluebook* format.

For Questions 4-6, use full-text search on *WestlawNext* or *Lexis Advance.* For your content on *WestlawNext,* you can limit your searches to Law Reviews & Journals in Secondary Sources. On *Lexis Advance,* you can filter by category. Select Secondary Materials.

4. Locate the 2013 South Texas Law Review article by Edward C. Lyons and provide the cite in proper *Bluebook* format.

5. Locate the 2015 William and Mary Law Review article that analyzes *Kubert v. Best,* 75 A.3d 1214 (N.J. Super. Ct. App. Div. 2013). Provide the cite in proper *Bluebook* format. **Note**: This article is student written.

6. Locate the 2010 Southern California Law Review article about punitive damages and saving lives. Provide the cite in proper *Bluebook* format.

Exercise F

For Questions 1-3, use one of the periodical indexes: *Index to Legal Periodicals, Current Law Index,* **or** *LegalTrac.* **Pull the article to cite it.**

1. Locate the 2002 William and Mary Law Review article by Edward A. Hartnett and provide the cite in proper *Bluebook* format.

2. Locate the 2002 Villanova Sports & Entertainment Law Journal article that analyzes *V Secret Catalogue, Inc. v. Moseley*, 259 F.3d 464 (6th Cir. 2002). Provide the cite in proper *Bluebook* format. **Note**: This article is student written.

3. Locate the 2002 Brigham Young University Journal of Public Law article about family policy and domestic relations. Provide the cite in proper *Bluebook* format.

For Questions 4-6, use full-text search on *WestlawNext* **or** *Lexis Advance.* **For your content on** *WestlawNext,* **you can limit your searches to Law Reviews & Journals in Secondary Sources. On** *Lexis Advance,* **you can filter by category. Select Secondary Materials.**

4. Locate the 2012 UCLA Law Review article by Amy Kapczynski and provide the cite in proper *Bluebook* format.

5. Locate the 2010 Pepperdine Law Review article that analyzes *Ashcroft v. Iqbal*, 556 U.S. 662 (2009). Provide the cite in proper *Bluebook* format. **Note**: This article is student written.

6. Locate the 2012 Ohio State Law Journal article about regulating workplace chemicals. Provide the cite in proper *Bluebook* format.

Assignment Fifteen
Chapter 19
TREATISES, RESTATEMENTS, UNIFORM LAWS, MODEL ACTS

GOAL:
• Provide practice using a treatise, Restatement, and uniform act.

CITATION:

♦ For purposes of Assignment Fifteen, assume you are citing the treatises and cases in citations in a legal document, and not in textual sentences. Consequently, follow the typeface conventions in Bluepages B2.

♦ Use *Bluebook* Rule 15 for citing books, reports, and other nonperiodic materials and Rule 12.9.4 to cite uniform acts.

♦ Use Rule 10 to cite cases. For case names, apply the abbreviation rules in 10.2.2 and use table T6. Tables T1 and T10 will also be useful. Unless specifically instructed to do so, do not include information as to prior or subsequent history weight of authority for cases.

♦ Even if you are not instructed to give the complete cite in proper *Bluebook* format, use *Bluebook* abbreviations in your answers.

SOURCES: **OTHER SOURCES:**

Print   **Online**

Questions 1-4:   *HeinOnline*
Dan B. Dobbs, *The Law of Torts* (2000).   *Bloomberg Law*

Questions 5–8:
Restatement (Second) of Contracts (1981).

Questions 9-10:
Uniform Laws Annotated, Master Edition

Online

Questions 5-8:
WestlawNext
Lexis Advance

Questions 9-10:
WestlawNext

EXAMPLE EXERCISE:

For Questions 1-4, refer to Dan B. Dobbs, *The Law of Torts* (2000).

1. According to the general rule, if an on-duty firefighter is injured while battling a blaze that was negligently set by a homeowner, does the firefighter have a claim against the homeowner?
   No

2. Provide the entire section that addressed Question 1.
   Section 285

3. Under the section from Question 2, locate the 1960 Supreme Court of New Jersey case that is considered a leading case on the "firefighters' rule." Provide the cite to the case in proper *Bluebook* format.
   ***Krauth v. Geller*, 157 A.2d 129 (N.J. 1960).**

4. Use the Table of Cases in the treatise. In what section and footnote is *Dykema v. King*, 959 F. Supp. 736 (D.S.C. 1997) cited?
   Section 256, n. 16

For Questions 5-8, refer to the *Restatement (Second) of Contracts* (1981). Do not consult the Appendices or pocket supplements.

5. John, while intoxicated, entered into a contract with Steve. Are John's contractual duties voidable if Steve knew at the time John entered into the contract he was too drunk to understand the nature and consequences of the contract? Look for the section that deals specifically with intoxicated persons.
   Yes

6. Provide the cite to the entire section that answers Question 5.
   Section 16

7. In the Reporter's Note for the section from Question 6, locate the 1954 Supreme Court of Virginia case where the court focused on the conduct of the non-intoxicated party and the fairness of the contract. Provide the cite to the case in proper *Bluebook* format.
    Lucy v. Zehmer, 84 S.E.2d 516 (Va. 1954).

8. Use Table V: Cases Cited in Reporter's Notes. In what section's Reporter's Note is *Adan v. Steinbrecher*, 133 N.W. 477 (Minn. 1911) cited?
    Section 169

For Questions 9-10, refer to the _Uniform Laws Annotated_ either in print or on _WestlawNext_.

9. Find the Uniform Alcoholism and Intoxication Treatment Act in the *Uniform Laws Annotated*. Provide the cite to the act in proper *Bluebook* format. NOTE: *WestlawNext* does not provide sufficient information to properly cite in *Bluebook* format.
    Unif. Alcoholism & Intoxication Treatment Act, 9 U.L.A. 225 (1971).

10. Has your state adopted the uniform law from Question 9?
    Answers will vary depending on your state.

Exercise A

For Questions 1-4, refer to Dan B. Dobbs, *The Law of Torts* (2000).

1. Under the contemporary general rule, does a landowner owe a responsibility of a duty of care to a five-year-old child who trespasses into the landowner's backyard and drowns in the unfenced swimming pool, if the landowner knows the child lived next door and the cost of erecting a fence was minimal?

2. Provide the entire section that addressed Question 1.

3. Under the section from Question 2, locate the 1967 Court of Appeals of Arizona case in which the court found the homeowner liable when the child was a five-year-old. Provide the cite to the case in proper *Bluebook* format.

4. Use the Table of Cases in the treatise. In what section and footnote is *Rich for Rich v. Kentucky Country Day, Inc.*, 793 S.W.2d 832 (Ky. Ct. App. 1990) cited?

For Questions 5-8, refer to the *Restatement (Second) of Contracts* (1981). Do not consult the Appendices or pocket supplements.

5. Stephanie and Abigail enter into a one-year contract for Abigail personally to transcribe Stephanie's memoirs. Does Abigail's death before the end of the year term result in "objective" impracticability?

6. Provide the cite to the entire section whose comment answers Question 5.

7. In the Reporter's Note for the section from Question 6, locate the 1967 Supreme Judicial Court of Massachusetts case that was the basis for Illustration 1. Provide the cite to the case in proper *Bluebook* format.

8. Use Table V: Cases Cited in Reporter's Notes. In what section's Reporter's Note is *Bauman v. McManus*, 89 P. 15 (Kan. 1907) cited?

For Questions 9-10, refer to the *Uniform Laws Annotated* either in print or on *WestlawNext*.

9. Find the Uniform Photographic Copies of Business and Public Records As Evidence Act in the *Uniform Laws Annotated*. Provide the cite to the act in proper *Bluebook* format. NOTE: *WestlawNext* does not provide sufficient information to properly cite in *Bluebook* format.

10. Has your state adopted the uniform law from Question 9?

Exercise B

For Questions 1-4, refer to Dan B. Dobbs, *The Law of Torts* (2000).

1. Does a player participating in an active, competitive sport such as football have a duty to avoid intentionally or recklessly injuring another player?

2. Provide the entire section that addressed Question 1.

3. Under the section from Question 2, locate the 1975 Court of Appeals of Illinois case that held that a deliberate, prohibited kick in soccer could be actionable under the standard in Question 1. Provide the cite to the case in proper *Bluebook* format.

4. Use the Table of Cases in the treatise. In what section and footnote is *Weil v. Seltzer*, 873 F.2d 1453 (D.C. Cir. 1989) cited?

For Questions 5-8, refer to the *Restatement (Second) of Contracts* (1981). Do not consult the Appendices or pocket supplements.

5. When looking at the parties required for a contract, must a contract have at least two parties, the promisor and promisee?

6. Provide the cite to the entire section that answers Question 5.

7. In the Reporter's Note for the section from Question 6, locate the 1974 Ninth Circuit case that states a person cannot contract with himself. Provide the cite to the case in proper *Bluebook* format.

8. Use Table V: Cases Cited in Reporter's Notes. In what section's Reporter's Note is *Clark v. Ingle*, 266 P.2d 672 (N.M. 1954) cited?

For Questions 9-10, refer to the *Uniform Laws Annotated* either in print or on *WestlawNext*.

9. Find the Uniform Comparative Fault Act in the *Uniform Laws Annotated*. Provide the cite to the act in proper *Bluebook* format. NOTE: *WestlawNext* does not provide sufficient information to properly cite in *Bluebook* format.

10. Has your state adopted the uniform law from Question 9?

Exercise C

For Questions 1-4, refer to Dan B. Dobbs, *The Law of Torts* (2000).

1. When a parent is libeled by another person, the parent can recover for the loss of esteem or standing in the eyes of the community and with friends and family. Do those damages include alienation of the child's affection?

2. Provide the entire section that addressed Question 1.

3. Under the section from Question 2, locate the 1995 Eastern District of Pennsylvania case that supports the answer in Question 1. Provide the cite to the case in proper *Bluebook* format.

4. Use the Table of Cases in the treatise. In what section and footnote is *Cornell v. Wunschel*, 408 N.W.2d 369 (Iowa 1987) cited?

For Questions 5-8, refer to the *Restatement (Second) of Contracts* (1981). Do not consult the Appendices or pocket supplements.

5. Paul enters into a personal service contract to paint George's portrait. Before Paul begins the project, he decides to forego the portrait and instead paint murals on a local business building. Can George force Paul to specifically perform under their contract and paint his portrait?

6. Provide the cite to the entire section that answers Question 5.

7. In the Reporter's Note for the section from Question 6, locate the 1963 Court of Appeals of Ohio case where the court refused specific performance of an employer's promise because personal supervision was involved. Provide the cite to the case in proper *Bluebook* format.

8. Use Table V: Cases Cited in Reporter's Notes. In what section's Reporter's Note is *Dunlop v. Mercer*, 156 F. 545 (8th Cir. 1907) cited?

For Questions 9-10, refer to the *Uniform Laws Annotated* either in print or on *WestlawNext*.

9. Find the Uniform Foreign-Money Claims Act in the *Uniform Laws Annotated*. Provide the cite to the act in proper *Bluebook* format. NOTE: *WestlawNext* does not provide sufficient information to properly cite in *Bluebook* format.

10. Has your state adopted the uniform law from Question 9?

Exercise D

For Questions 1-4, refer to Dan B. Dobbs, *The Law of Torts* (2000).

1. What is the standard of care that lawyers owe their clients so as not to be liable for malpractice?

2. Provide the entire section that addressed Question 1.

3. Under the section from Question 2, locate the 1997 Supreme Court of Arkansas case that held attorneys are not liable for good faith errors of judgment. Provide the cite to the case in proper *Bluebook* format.

4. Use the Table of Cases in the treatise. In what section and footnote is *Adkins v. Dixon*, 482 S.E.2d 797 (Va. 1997) cited?

For Questions 5-8, refer to the *Restatement (Second) of Contracts* (1981). Do not consult the Appendices or pocket supplements.

5. Mary Beth is attending an auction where items are put up for bid without reserve. The auctioneer has started the bidding for a classic Corvette at $5,000.00. At the end of the bidding, Mary Beth has placed the highest bid of $15,000.00, well under the market price for the car. Under the rules for auctions, must the auction house sell the car to Mary Beth?

6. Provide the cite to the entire section that answers Question 5.

7. In the Reporter's Note for the section from Question 6, locate the 1976 Court of Appeals of Missouri case that pertains to Illustration 5. Provide the cite to the case in proper *Bluebook* format.

8. Use Table V: Cases Cited in Reporter's Notes. In what section's Reporter's Note is *Ingham Lumber Co. v. Ingersoll*, 125 S.W. 139 (Ark. 1910) cited?

For Questions 9-10, refer to the *Uniform Laws Annotated* either in print or on *WestlawNext*.

9. Find the Uniform Athlete Agents Act in the *Uniform Laws Annotated*. Provide the cite to the act in proper *Bluebook* format. NOTE: WestlawNext does not provide sufficient information to properly cite in Bluebook format.

10. Has your state adopted the uniform law from Question 9?

Exercise E

For Questions 1-4, refer to Dan B. Dobbs, *The Law of Torts* (2000).

1. Under a state's Good Samaritan statute, is a doctor who stops on the way to the grocery store to render medical aid to a person severely injured in an automobile accident liable for medical negligence?

2. Provide the entire section that addressed Question 1.

3. Under the section from Question 2, locate the 1991 Court of Appeals of California case that extended the Good Samaritan rule beyond emergency scene and applied it to a surgeon operating in a hospital operating room. Provide the cite to the case in proper *Bluebook* format.

4. Use the Table of Cases in the treatise. In what section and footnote is *Kleinschmidt v. Morrow*, 642 A.2d 161 (Me. 1994) cited?

For Questions 5-8, refer to the *Restatement (Second) of Contracts* (1981). Do not consult the Appendices or pocket supplements.

5. Mason owes Kyle $500.00 from a debt incurred six months ago. Last week, Mason filed for bankruptcy. Today, Mason promised Kyle he would pay her the money he owed her even though the $500.00 could be discharged in bankruptcy. Is Mason's promise to pay Kyle binding?

6. Provide the cite to the entire section that answers Question 5.

7. In the Reporter's Note for the section from Question 6, locate the 1967 Court of Appeals of Georgia case that pertains to Comment a. Provide the cite to the case in proper *Bluebook* format.

8. Use Table V: Cases Cited in Reporter's Notes. In what section's Reporter's Note is *Leasco Corp. v. Taussig*, 473 F.2d 777 (2d Cir. 1972) cited?

For Questions 9-10, refer to the *Uniform Laws Annotated* either in print or on *WestlawNext*.

9. Find the Uniform Marital Property Act in the *Uniform Laws Annotated*. Provide the cite to the act in proper *Bluebook* format. NOTE: *WestlawNext* does not provide sufficient information to properly cite in *Bluebook* format.

10. Has your state adopted the uniform law from Question 9?

Exercise F

For Questions 1-4, refer to Dan B. Dobbs, *The Law of Torts* (2000).

1. In order to succeed on a claim of libel or slander, must the plaintiff prove that the defendant published defamatory material about the plaintiff?

2. Provide the entire section that addressed Question 1.

3. Under the section from Question 2, locate the 1914 Supreme Judicial Court of Massachusetts case that held publication does not include words spoken in a foreign language to someone who does not understand the foreign language. Provide the cite to the case in proper *Bluebook* format.

4. Use the Table of Cases in the treatise. In what section and footnote is *Peterson v. Shields*, 652 S.W.2d 929 (Tex. 1983) cited?

For Questions 5-8, refer to the *Restatement (Second) of Contracts* (1981). Do not consult the Appendices or pocket supplements.

5. Peter and Sally make a valid oral contract. Peter then writes a memorandum that memorializes the terms of their agreement. Instead of using his name as the signature on memorandum, Peter signs with a peace sign, the symbol he has recently adopted to authenticate his writings. Is this peace sign the type to be a valid signature?

6. Provide the cite to the entire section that answers Question 5.

7. In the Reporter's Note for the section from Question 6, locate the 1927 Court of Appeals of New York case that is the basis for Illustration 1. Provide the cite to the case in proper *Bluebook* format.

8. Use Table V: Cases Cited in Reporter's Notes. In what section's Reporter's Note is *Oxley v. Ralston Purina Co.*, 349 F.2d 328 (6th Cir. 1965) cited?

For Questions 9-10, refer to the *Uniform Laws Annotated* either in print or on *WestlawNext*.

9. Find the Uniform Parentage Act (2000) in the *Uniform Laws Annotated*. Provide the cite to the act in proper *Bluebook* format. NOTE: *WestlawNext* does not provide sufficient information to properly cite in *Bluebook* format.

10. Has your state adopted the uniform law from Question 9?

RESEARCH PROBLEMS

GOALS:
• To put together the research skills you have learned in previous assignments.
• To research specific fact situations.

CITATIONS:

♦**For purposes of Assignment Sixteen, assume you are researching for a memorandum of law. Consequently, follow the typeface conventions for citations in Bluepages B2.**

INSTRUCTIONS:
These exercises provide practice in putting together the skills you have learned in the previous assignments.

Possible Steps:
1. **Read and analyze the problem.**
   - T—Thing or subject matter
   - A—Cause of action or ground of defense
   - R—Relief sought; and
   - P—Persons or parties involved in the problem

2. **Formulate the legal issues to be researched.**
   Look at secondary sources (law reviews, legal encyclopedias, A.L.R. annotations) to get an overview and leads on cases and statutes.

3. **Begin your research of primary law with one of the following:**
   Read the cases and/or statutes located in the secondary sources;
   Locate cases relevant to your problem; or
   Locate statutes relevant to your problem.

4. **Expand your research:**
   If you have a relevant case, find additional cases using a relevant topic and Key number.
   If you have a relevant statute, look at the cases that interpret that statute.

5. **Update your law:**
   For cases, use a citator to verify your case is good law and to see any relevant negative treatment.
   For statutes, make sure you are using the most current statute or the statute that was applicable at the time of the cause of action.

Exercise A[1]

After a whirl-wind courtship filled with passions in the city of Santa Barbara, Beauregarde and Faith Brady were married in November 2007. Beau had three grown children from a previous marriage. In February 2011, Beau, a doctor at General Hospital in Port Charles, decided that he was no longer one of the young and the restless and that the time had come to execute a will. Being somewhat frugal, Beau decided to forego hiring an attorney to draft the document. Instead, Beau wrote the following will in his own handwriting:

I, Beauregarde Brady, being of sound mind and health do hereby declare that this is my last will and testament. My loving family, if you are reading this will then I have obviously followed the guiding light to another world. To you I bequeath the following: To the bold and the beautiful Faith, for her generous support all the days of our lives, I leave my entire estate, including all property, real and personal, minus a token amount for each of my three children. To all my children, I leave you each $1,000 and these words of wisdom--You only have one life to live, so live each day to the fullest.

Beau signed and dated the document and then placed it in his safe.

On June 4, 2015, Beau Brady met with a tragic death when the single-engine Cessna he was piloting to Sunset Beach crashed on takeoff. The preliminary NTSB investigation is looking at pilot error as the cause of the crash since investigators found Beau had worked the night shift on four consecutive days from May 31 through June 3 and was probably suffering from great fatigue. His entire family was devastated by the event. However, when the contents of the will became known, his children were outraged that they were left a pittance and their stepmother inherited the bulk of the estate. They have challenged the validity of the will particularly since there were no witnesses and it was handwritten except for one typewritten provision, the last sentence (*To all my children, I leave you each $1,000 and these words of wisdom--You only have one life to live, so live each day to the fullest.*). Research the applicable law in your jurisdiction to determine if the will or any part of it is valid.

Note: All of the events in this problem took place in your jurisdiction.

---

[1] Problem reprinted with permission from Susan T. Phillips. Copyright 2015 by Susan T. Phillips.

<u>Exercise B</u>[2]

Until recently, Professor J.W. Hurney was a linguistics professor at the University of Verbiage, a highly-respected institution of higher education known for its strict academic standards. During his ten years at the University, Professor Hurney worked diligently day and night on what he considered to be the definitive work on improving the vocabulary of elementary school children in the Midwest. Finally, after years of research and writing, *Word Wealth for the West* was published. Fortunately for Professor Hurney, the book was an incredible success garnering kudos from around the educational and literary communities. In fact, the work's popularity was so great that Professor Hurney was asked to create an educational television series based on his work. The author jumped at the chance to be a part of such a creative and valuable project and tendered his resignation with the University.

The University of Verbiage was quite upset with losing such a valuable asset to their faculty. In fact, a few renegade professors, in a fit of jealousy, circulated a petition stating that the University was the true copyright owner of the work since Professor Hurney was an employee at the time of the writing of the book and calling for all proceeds from book sales to be given to the University since Hurney was required to write the work under the University's "publish or perish" policy. The University is now investigating whether Hurney or the University is the copyright owner of the work. The University's Faculty Handbook is silent on the issue of copyright ownership but does have a publication requirement for tenure. Research and determine whether Hurney or the University is the copyright owner under the applicable law in your jurisdiction.

Note: All of the events in this problem took place in your jurisdiction.

---

[2] Problem reprinted with permission from Susan T. Phillips. Copyright 2015 by Susan T. Phillips.

Exercise C[3]

Tina Rickles has come to our law firm seeking advice for a legal situation involving her young son, Eddie. Ms. Rickles has related the following information concerning the problem: Ms. Rickles met Tom Corbett on October 14, 2009. The two shared many common interests and soon a romantic relationship developed. The couple tried unsuccessfully for over a year to have a child. After seeing several fertility specialists, Tom and Tina conceived a child through artificial insemination using Tom's sperm and Tina's egg. They agreed that they were going to raise their child together. With Tom present, Tina gave birth to Eddie Corbett on December 30, 2012. The two were ecstatic over the birth of their child. The couple never married but did live together. Tom provided Eddie with financial support as well as paternal emotional support. Tom always referred to Eddie as his "son" whenever speaking of the child in conversation.

During the entire time of the above relationship, Tom Corbett was married to Crissy Drummond. Tom and Crissy met in 1976 and subsequently married on December 1, 1978. The couple never had children. On January 27, 1986 after years of work, Tom's novel *People Let Me Tell You About My Best Friend* was published by FWT Publishing Co. Tom retained all intellectual property rights to the novel. The book was a huge commercial success making it to the top of the *New York Times* Best Seller list and garnering many literary prizes. The work continues to sell briskly as it is often required reading in high school and undergraduate English courses.

In April 2009, Tom and Crissy came to the realization that they had grown apart as a couple and amicably agreed that each was free to enter into other relationships. The couple never bothered to divorce.

On March 14, 2015, Tom Corbett died tragically in a single car accident when he lost control of his convertible Corvette and hit a telephone pole. Everyone was devastated by the event, particularly Tom's housekeeper Mrs. Livingston. Since Tom's death, Crissy, Tom's widow, has been collecting the royalties from his book. Tina wants our law firm's help in obtaining Eddie's share of the royalties. Please research the applicable law to determine if Eddie is entitled to any of the royalties from Tom's book.

Note: All of the events in this problem took place in your jurisdiction.

---

[3] Problem reprinted with permission from Susan T. Phillips. Copyright 2015 by Susan T. Phillips.

Exercise D[4]

Marion Cunningham seeks our law firm's advice. She has given the following information: Marion married Howard Cunningham on November 14, 1976. Coincidentally, the spouses shared the same birthday, January 7, 1946. The couple had three adult children: Chuck, their ever-elusive eldest son; Richie, who is a successful Hollywood film director; and Joanie, their youngest who is now Mrs. Charles Arcola. In 1978, Howard sold the hardware store he had inherited from his father and went to work for TRX Rails, a railroad company, as a train engineer. Howard worked at TRX Rails until his retirement in February 2011 at age 65. Howard's monthly retirement pension was $2,510.00.

The first months of Howard's retirement were quite enjoyable for Marion and her husband. They traveled to see their children and grandchildren except Chuck, of course. Howard worked several times a week on reducing his golf handicap. In June 2011, the Cunninghams took a cruise to Alaska, a life-long dream for Marion. Unfortunately, their golden years did not last long. Howard was diagnosed with cancer in November 2013. On February 28, 2014, Howard died.

Marion was devastated by the loss. Immediately upon Howard's death, Marion applied for and began receiving survivor benefits of $1,020.00 per month from Howard's railroad pension. Marion sought support from a grief recovery support group and attended the group meetings faithfully. At the August 2014 meeting, Marion met Warren Weber, who told Marion that he had recently lost his wife in a terrible car accident. Marion and Warren quickly became inseparable. After a brief courtship, the two obtained a marriage license on December 29, 2014 and were wed on December 31, 2014, much to the chagrin of the Cunningham children, except Chuck, of course. With Marion's new marriage came the cessation of the survivor benefits she had been receiving.

Alas, Marion's happiness was not to be. On January 22, 2014, Marion was shocked to learn that Warren was having a secret affair he initiated on January 1, 2014 with Jennifer, his high school sweetheart. Marion immediately kicked Warren out of their residence and had the locks changed.

Marion is in quite a quandary. She wants nothing else to do with Warren. Thus, she finds herself seeking our legal advice. Marion wants to know if there is a way to dissolve the marriage so that the pension will be revived AND what effect such possible marital dissolution would have on the revival of the pension.

Note: All of the events in this problem took place in your jurisdiction.

---

[4] Problem reprinted with permission from Susan T. Phillips. Copyright 2015 by Susan T. Phillips.

Exercise E[5]

Ward Cleaver has retained our firm to represent him in his Chapter 7 bankruptcy case. Ward has been married to June Cleaver since 1979 and they have two grown sons Wallace and Theodore. Beginning in 1978, Ward served in the United States Navy until his retirement in 2005. He receives military retirement pay of $5,016.00 per month. In 2005, Ward decided to open and run his own bagel shop, Beaver's Bagels. Sales at the shop were extremely brisk for many years. The shop provided the Cleavers with an extremely lucrative income and they took full advantage of it. In 2007, the Cleavers purchased a $1.5 million home. The following year, the Cleavers purchased a vacation home in Kaneohe, Hawaii. The Cleavers belong to the local country club and are known for hosting lavish parties. The couple takes annual oversees vacations to very exotic destinations. Ward has been known to surprise June with extravagant gifts of jewelry for no particular reason. Ward drives a 2014 BMW and June drives a 2015 Lexus. Ward also solely owns (not June and not the business) a van that is used exclusively for Beaver's Bagels to make bagel deliveries to their contractual clients. The vehicle is a 2012 Ford Econoline E250 cargo van in good condition with 28,000 miles. The van had been purchased new for cash.

On July 1, 2014, June's father Howard Fitzhugh died of complications from a stroke that he had suffered back in October 2013. In Mr. Fitzhugh's valid and uncontested will, he bequeathed his prized Spanish gold 1964 Mustang "to my darling daughter June Cleaver for all of your years of love and devotion." In addition, Mr. Fitzhugh left $60,000.00 "to Ward and June Cleaver."

Unfortunately, Beaver's Bagels business has been in rapid decline over the past two years. The Cleavers are completely over-extended; consequently, Ward decided to file for bankruptcy. On August 15, 2015, Ward filed for voluntary, personal Chapter 7 bankruptcy.

Several associates are working on this case. The senior partner has asked you to research the law and let her know how each of the following will be treated as to the bankruptcy estate:

1. The $5,016.00 monthly military retirement pay
2. The Ford Econoline E250 cargo van
3. The Spanish gold 1964 Mustang
4. The $60,000 inheritance

Note: All of the events in this problem took place in your jurisdiction.

---

[5] Problem reprinted with permission from Susan T. Phillips. Copyright 2015 by Susan T. Phillips.

Exercise F[6]

On November 14, 2007, 45-year-old Robert Dallam married 20-year-old Beatrice Honeycutt. Since obtaining his MBA, Robert had been employed at International Falcone, Ltd. In 2009, Robert was promoted to vice-president with a salary of 300,000 for the year plus was granted $50,000 in stock options under an employer plan to buy stock in the employer. Each subsequent year, Robert received a 10% raise in his salary but no more stock options. Beatrice was a domestic engineer with a high school diploma. Beatrice never participated in doing the family finances, leaving Robert to pay all of the bills and balance the checkbook for their joint checking account.

In January 2009, the Dallams purchased a house worth $585,000 at 13456 Burning Log Lane as their residence and lived relatively modestly considering their income. They both drove Honda Accords and took only a one-week vacation per year; however, they were members of a local country club.

For every year of their marriage, the Dallams filed a joint income tax return beginning in April 2008. Robert did their taxes himself. Not having any financial experience nor contributing any income, Beatrice simply signed the return each year. Unbeknownst to Beatrice, Robert cashed in his stock options in 2010. He made a $60,000 profit (ordinary compensation income under I.R.S. Code § 423) which he secretly gave to his adult son Stephen Dallam for Stephen's down payment on a house. Robert never reported the money as income on his 2010 income tax return filed on April 15, 2011.

On May 15, 2012, the Dallams received notice and demand from the Internal Revenue Service ("I.R.S.") concerning the deficiency of the $60,000 income (there is no dispute that the $60,000 is income) on their 2010 Federal Income Tax Return. Robert told Beatrice he would take care of the matter; however, on December 30, 2012, Robert died in a tragic car accident before rectifying the I.R.S. matter. Subsequently, the I.R.S. has placed a lien on the house.

Our firm has been hired by Beatrice Dallam, who is concerned with the federal tax debt and the possibility of the I.R.S. foreclosing the federal tax lien on the Burning Log residence and forcing the sale of the house to satisfy the debt.
Please thoroughly research the substantive law concerning Beatrice Dallam's legal problems. Assume that the I.R.S. lien was properly perfected and all procedural issues including statutes of limitation are not at issue, nor is Stephen's house.

Note: All of the events in this problem took place in your jurisdiction.

---

[6] Problem reprinted with permission from Susan T. Phillips. Copyright 2015 by Susan T. Phillips.